LOOKING THROUGH MY

MOTHER'S EYES

PICAS SERIES 38

Guernica Editions Inc. acknowledges the support
of The Canada Council for the Arts.
Guernica Editions Inc. acknowledges the support
of the Ontario Arts Council.
Guernica Editions Inc. acknowledges the Government of Ontario
through the Ontario Media Development Corporation's
Ontario Book Initiative.
Guernica Editions Inc. acknowledges the financial support
of the Government of Canada through the Book Publishing Industry
Development Program (BPIDP).

GIOVANNA DEL NEGRO

LOOKING THROUGH MY MOTHER'S EYES

LIFE STORIES OF NINE ITALIAN IMMIGRANT
WOMEN IN CANADA

GUERNICA

TORONTO · BUFFALO · CHICAGO · LANCASTER (U.K.)

2003

Antonio D'Alfonso, Editor.
Guernica Editions, Inc.
P.O. Box 117, Station P, Toronto (Ontario), Canada M5S 2S6
2250 Military Road, Tonawanda, N.Y. 14150-6000 U.S.A.

Distributors:
University of Toronto Press Distribution,
5201 Dufferin Street, Toronto, (ON), Canada M3H 5T8

Gazelle Book Services, Falcon House, Queen Square,
Lancaster LA1 1RN U.K.

Independent Publishers Group,
814 N. Franklin Street, Chicago, Il. 60610 U.S.A.

Second edition.
Legal Deposit – First Quarter
National Library of Canada

Library of Congress Catalogue Card Number: 2003102472.
National Library of Canada Cataloguing in Publication
National Library of Canada Cataloguing in Publication
Del Negro, Giovanna
Looking through my mother's eyes :
life stories of nine Italian immigrant women in Canada /
Giovanna Del Negro. – 2nd ed.
Includes bibliographical references.
ISBN 1-55071-174-1
1. Italian-Canadian women–Biography.
2. Italian-Canadian women–Folklore.
3. Italian-Canadian women–Social conditions.
4. Women immigrants–Canada–Biography.
5. Women immigrants–Canada–Folklore.
6. Women immigrants–Canada–Social conditions.
I. Title. II. Series: Picas series ; 38.
GR470.D45   2003   305.48'851071   C2003-901156-9

CONTENTS

NOTE TO THE SECOND EDITION

In the years since the first publication of this book much has changed for Italian immigrants in Canada. A sizable minority of Italian immigrants and their children have returned to Italy, and some of the items of folklore discussed in these pages have begun to circulate less frequently in the oral tradition. A number of the women who participated in this study (including Gino Lorenzo and Francesca Mancini) have died. While there have been positive changes in the gender roles of Italian ethnic women in Canada, many of the cultural and gender dynamics I have outlined here still play out in the experiences of women. I believe this book not only documents an important moment in the social history of ethnic Canada, but that it illustrates some of the complex ways in which folklore and gender become intertwined in women's lives.

I dedicate this second printing of the book to all of the women who generously shared their time with me and have since passed away.

G.D.N.
February, 2003

SCENES FROM THE KITCHEN

An Autobiographical Note

As a young child I was fascinated with the parade of characters who came to life around the kitchen table during my relatives' ritual Sunday visits. Although the male presence was not absent from these occasions, women often dominated them. Since it was customary to greet relatives and sit with them at the table, I frequently became a captive audience, hearing an assortment of stories ranging from family lore to gossip. At first I resented having to sit through what I thought was useless banter, but I later learned to appreciate the skillful storytelling and animated interactions of these sessions.

In the span of several hours, over coffee, amaretto cookies and liqueur, the kitchen was transformed into a dramatic stage where issues of motherhood, work, immigration and marriage were examined through stories. The simple act of talking revealed a complex tapestry of meanings.

It was in this context that I became familiar with the expressive style of speech and performance that women in my community used. The classic stories usually involved either unmarried village girls who defied authority and accomplished their goals through cleverness, or savvy older women who used their sharp tongues to their best advantage.

The dialogue was sometimes peppered with obscene language, bawdy repartee and ritual insults which became more and more absurd as the conversation unfolded.

Today my fascination with Italian immigrant women's folklore stems from the fact that the women who told these stories were, by definition, the respectable tradition bearers of the community. They were not by any means self-proclaimed feminists or self-conscious innovators. Yet the symbolic personae that emerged during such events seemed to clash with their established roles. It is with these women in mind that I wrote this book. These women's voices, images and characters people my imagination and tug at my memory. This book, in some small way, pays homage to the legacy that Italian immigrant women have left to the younger generation of Italian-Canadian women like myself. To them, the women whose lives I describe in this study and my parents, Anna and Giovanni Del Negro, I dedicate this book.

I am deeply indebted to the women who took time to share their life stories with me. Their contributions are invaluable to furthering the knowledge of the experiences of immigrant women. Many thanks go to the coordinator of Centro Donne, Linda Azzuolo, who provided assistance and advice regarding potential candidates for interviewing. I am also grateful to Paul J. Perry for the photographs which complement this research.

This book is largely based on my thesis, *Life Stories of Italian-Canadian Women*, which I wrote in 1989 at Bowling Green State University in partial fulfillment of my Masters degree in Popular Culture. I greatly appreciate the direction, criticism and insight provided by my committee members Marilyn Motz and Jack Santino. Gratitude is also expressed to Karen Gould. During my studies at Indiana University's Folklore Institute, Professor Sandra Dolby's direction has been of key importance. Her scholarship and confidence greatly encouraged my intellectual development as a Ph.D. student. My conversations with professors Richard Bauman, John Bodnar, Henry Glassie and John Johnson have also been invigorating and enlightening.

Special thanks to my husband, Harris M. Berger, whose kind support, editorial comments and assistance made this task less daunting. I am extremely lucky to have a sharp critical thinker as a colleague and partner. I would also like to extend my thanks to anthropology professor Donna Coppola-Budani at the University of Delaware for her insightful comments and suggestions. Our conversations energized me at the moments I needed it most. I would also like to thank Amanda Cicarelli, Franca Iacovetta, Jennifer Livesay and Paolo Villa with their help on an earlier draft. I am also indebted to my friends Emilia, Francesca, Maria and Theresa for their unwavering encouragement and friendship. Our shared backgrounds and frequent conversations provide the critical ground for this book. I am grateful to Ur and Mano for their cheer and good humor. Their charm and wit lifted my spirits.

Lastly, I want to express special thanks to my

editor, Antonio D'Alfonso, for his comments and
support in bringing this project to fruition.

CHAPTER ONE

Introduction

This collection of life stories from nine Italian-Canadian women explores the highly neglected topic of women's activities and folklore. In daily life, popular culture and academic writing, men's experiences and ideas are taken as the norm and women are pushed to the margins or made invisible.[1] In these life stories, the immigrant woman takes center stage. No longer an adjunct to the male experience,[2] these "women of the shadows"[3] emerge from their silence to speak in their own voices about their hopes, dreams and struggles.

Because everyday life is the raw material from which people create knowledge, we stand to gain new understandings and new visions of social life by turning our attention to the life stories of these nine women. Most importantly, these women's lives clearly show how knowledge and meaning grow out of everyday experience as much as they arise from the ivory towers of academia.

This study focuses on the life experiences of nine Italian women who immigrated to Montreal, Quebec. The youngest in the group is forty-three while the eldest is eighty-five. Most of the women received little formal schooling, except for learning to sew (*il mestiere*). They joined spouses or came to Canada with family members during the latter part of the 1950s or 1960s. Some were married and had families, while others came as single women and later married Italian men from their neighborhoods. Fleeing harsh living conditions (*la miseria*[4]), these women, like countless other Italians, left their homeland seeking a better way of life.

In telling their life stories the women that I spoke with expressed resentment and ambivalence toward the repressive cultural values and practices that limited and sometimes dictated their choice of husbands and activities. In framing and reframing their life experiences as women, mothers and workers, they simultaneously affirmed and challenged patriarchal beliefs.

A social commentary and introspective dialogue about being female in a male-dominated society, the narratives also speak of the ways in which women subverted their socially prescribed roles by engaging in taboo behavior among themselves at home or at work in the predominantly gender-segregated environment of the textile factory. Above all, we see how women stretched the boundaries of their culture, finding ways of criticizing the status quo without openly calling into question the fundamental values of their society.

The first chapter provides a review of academic research in several fields. Feminist scholarship is explored, and an outline of traditional Italian society is presented; the chapter also discusses contemporary approaches to the study of the life story and the personal narrative. The second chapter consists of summaries and interpretations of the women's life stories interspersed with brief descriptions of the settings in which the interviews took place. The last chapter begins by examining the women's life stories, with particular attention to their discussion of the repressive practice of forced seclusion. The chapter ends by revealing how the women creatively responded to such cultural constraints through songs, lullabies, riddles and trickster tales.

While the life stories of Stefania Annibale, Filomena Azzuolo, Giuseppina Barbuci, Antonietta De Fronzo, Anna Del Negro (my mother), Genoveffa Della Zazzera, Graziella Di Corpo, Gina Lorenzo and Francesca Mancini together make up a complex text capable of many readings,[5] I hope that their words offer insights into how subordinate groups have developed, and continue to develop, creative survival strategies for coping with repressive social conditions.

Previous Explorations

Four scholarly literatures have shaped my thinking about Italian-Canadian women and their life stories. For the graduate student, a review of this kind helps him/her to situate research interests within a broader academic setting; it provides the opportunity to stand on the shoulders of academic foremothers and forefathers and pay tribute to their achievements. For the general reader, however, such a review is equally important because it connects the study to the burning issues and questions of the day. For both the audience and the reader, this alternately tedious and exhilarating task aligns our thinking with others and helps clarify, refine and focus our thoughts on the subject at hand. Perhaps the most enjoyable part of this exercise is that it generates countless questions about human experience, questions which ultimately defy neat theoretical explanations.

The research literature that we are about to examine has significantly enhanced my understanding of women and their lives; each section brings particular concerns and issues to bear on the subject. The feminist writing on this topic, for example, has sensitized me to the complex and often undervalued experiences of women's lives, especially those of immigrant women. This perspective redresses an academic imbalance by treating women's experiences as worthy of study. I have also included a brief section on traditional Italian society to provide an historical backdrop with which to understand the social climate of post World War II Italy.

The section on life story research explores how people craft tales of their past as part of an existential project to create meaning in the present. From this perspective, the life story is seen to stem from the creative process by which the human imagination confers coherence upon the sometimes disconnected and arbitrary events that make up a lifetime.

Similarly, the discussion of the personal narrative literature examines how stories of everyday life are embedded with powerful symbolic meanings, meanings which invoke the past and become richer each time they are retold. These narratives of the quotidian are extraordinarily revealing, as they provide glimpses into the musings of the human soul.

Before turning to the research literature, one final note. The word *folklore* is used throughout this study, and, as an Italian-Canadian folklorist, I feel a duty to explain what I mean by this heavily contested term. In my view, the discipline of folklore is devoted to the study of the aesthetics of everyday life[6] and the ways ordinary people artfully create meaning through daily interactions. The rich expressive behavior that is the stuff of folklore includes stories, riddles, proverbs, dances, customs, rituals, crafts and all manner of beliefs and practices – beliefs and practices that frequently occur on the margins of power. From my perspective, almost any kind of physical object or social activity that has been touched and transformed by the human spirit can be considered folklore.[7]

Feminist Perspective

In recent years there has been an emerging interest in the experiences of ethnic women. However, even with the latest trends in academic research, there is little work that examines the experiences of Italian-Canadian women.

Only in the last few years has the folklore dealing with women's activities achieved a legitimate place in the discipline. Until recently, folklore research has denigrated women's expressive behavior, referring to it as "women's talk" or "old wives tales."[8] Although in Western society women's roles are no longer confined to the home, many specifically female forms of folklore are transmitted in intimate surroundings, often in situations to which only women are privy. Studies have shown that, while men were typically found in the public sphere talking on street corners and in general stores, women were found talking behind closed doors.[9] The tendency in academic discourse has been to "marginalize the private and domestic realm placing it outside of history."[10]

The male bias in folklore studies has excluded the experiences of women from academic discourse; however, more and more scholars are becoming sensitive to issues of gender and how gender shapes human experience. With the increasing interest in women's personal experience narratives (stories of everyday events), conversational style and oral histories, some challenging interpretations are being presented. In a feminist analysis of women's speech, Joan N. Radner and Susan S. Lanser[11] argue that women's subordinate position within the power structure has led them to develop different communication strategies from men. These scholars suggest that women's expressive styles conceal different levels of meaning, often hiding subversive messages of protest against the established order.

Current feminist analysis in this area tries to

uncover the covert ways in which women have managed to speak through and with the constraints and limitations of patriarchal structures. Many studies demonstrate how women use traditional forms of expression to express non traditional messages. Italian folklorist Alessandro Falassi points out how Tuscan lullabies express hostile attitudes about motherhood.[12] Here, the soothing and melodic tunes frequently draw attention away from lyrics which speak of the desire to be liberated from the burdens of motherhood. In such a way, feelings of frustration and resentment are expressed and the role of the mother, highly revered in Italian culture, is indirectly criticized.

Within the same gender-informed framework, many scholars suggest that a large part of women's culture has been overlooked because of the taboo content of certain personal narratives. For instance, obscene joke telling and bantering is known to exist among women. In the past these kinds of female verbal genres have been understudied, because women are less likely to participate in this type of irreverent behavior in the presence of a male researcher; such expressive activity is almost exclusively reserved for women. Likewise male researchers are probably less inclined to ask about female specific lore. Ultimately, the web of meanings which emerge through such verbal interactions are filtered through the lens of gender, ethnicity, social class and situational context. Given all these factors, there is a great deal of data that has been left unexplored or inadequately covered.

Traditional Italian Society

The vast regional differences that exists in Italy, along with the paucity of information concerning the experiences of Italian immigrant women, make it difficult to provide a comprehensive and fair assessment of Old World beliefs and practices. Given these limitations, however, I will present a thumbnail sketch of traditional Italian society.[13] This is mainly for the purpose of giving the reader a context, albeit incomplete, in which to view the Italian immigrant woman. The first part consists of a brief critical overview of the diverging interpretations that exist within the scant literature. The second part gives some background data concerning the prevailing family values, lifestyles and class system in traditional Italian culture.

In reviewing the fragmentary studies that touch upon the Italian woman's socialization, role in the family, work experience and other related activities, one encounters divergent interpretations. From a North American perspective, when we consider the Italian woman we picture a passively subservient, uneducated, family-oriented person. Though an inaccurate stereotype, in a sense, this image describes the subordinate position of women in a patriarchal and authoritarian milieu.

There are many Italian proverbial sayings that attest to women's secondary status in Italian culture, but once a woman becomes a mother, her role is changed and she is revered as the "stabilizing, unifying force of the family."[14] The mother figure has been "so extolled in Italy" that some observers term

Italian culture as one of "motherolotry."[15] In contrast, historian Vincenza Scarpaci believes that such perceptions perpetuate a unidimensional vision of Italian women's varied experiences.

Rejecting the simplistic characterization by historians of the Italian woman as peasant (*contadina*), Scarpaci argues that the scarce literature on the subject "falls short of documenting women's history in a way that illustrates women's full participation in and interaction with their various worlds."[16] This position has been echoed by other historians, whose work on Italian immigrant women in North American tries to represent the diversity of women's worlds by showing many different settings, ranging from the orchard and the field to the home.[17] Overall, the majority of immigration history has tended to neglect the "uglier" side of Italian immigration, choosing to stress the "resiliency" of immigrant families.[18] While Italian immigrant women survived the strains of the immigration process, one historian reminds us that "we ought not forget that this was sometimes achieved at great emotional cost."[19]

With these general considerations in place, I now turn to some specific details of traditional Italian culture. According to sociologist Herbert Gans's classic work on an Italian neighborhood in Boston, *The Urban Villagers*, traditional Italian society is made of four major strata rigidly separated by a social hierarchy.[20] They were as follows:

> 1. the gentry (*galantuomini*), including the nobility, other large landowners, the professionals and the clergy;

2. the artisans (*artigiani*), including craftsmen and small shopkeepers;

3. the peasants (*contadini*) who owned or leased tiny plots of land, and;

4. the day laborers (*giornalieri*) who each day looked for work on the estates and were rarely employed more than a third of the year.

Italian anthropologist Tullio Tentori's study of class and family in the town of Matera identified similar social rankings, along with strict traditional norms prohibiting marriage between members of the dominant and subordinate groups.[21] In this context, mixing with members of another class implied betrayal of class-linked values and beliefs.[22]

Studies on southern peasant women show that marriage was a contractual agreement between families, often motivated by economic factors.[23] Rarely was the choice of a marriage partner made directly "by the parties concerned."[24] Young men were kept far away from girls by a "barrier of taboos and social prejudices";[25] love was not a consideration in these matters,[26] and marriage, in some ways, merely meant escape from the father's tutelage.[27] The dowry was also an important bargaining tool for the potential bride. It was insurance for familial well-being and security.[28]

Even though, by custom, it was acceptable for men to exercise authority over their wives and children, scholars have pointed out that the mother "dominated the family."[29] Gans has observed that women in Italian-American culture tend to have greater verbal proficiency than men. He suggests that, because of the patriarchal system, women have had to develop covert means of subverting male authority. "Talk," says Gans, "is the woman's weapon for reducing inequalities in power between [men] and [women]."[30]

With respect to sexual mores, women were often supervised and seldom allowed outside the home unaccompanied, though there was variation in how strictly families enforced these unwritten laws.[31] The prevailing attitude was that women needed to be guarded because they were particularly helpless in the face of temptation.[32]

As in most of Mediterranean culture, honor played a very important role in the community.[33] This value might be more meaningful to protect in a small town where there is a great deal of face-to-face interaction.[34] Preserving one's reputation in this situation is a matter of practical utility. Scholars have observed that in Italian culture the female is closely tied to the concept of honor. One of the more effective ways of attacking the honor of the other, according to historian Harriet Perry, is by slurring the character of the females of the other's line. Perry argues that the strongest of these insults will pertain to the "mother's or sister's illicit sexual behavior."[35]

Life Story

Recent studies on the life story have emphasized the meanings people attribute to their life experiences. This perspective views the sharing of reminiscences and personal experience as an active, meaning-making process which involves both the creativity of the narrator and the researcher; the life history is a joint production.[36]

In emphasizing the creativity that goes into recollecting past experiences, events and feelings, some scholars have suggested that the life story is a blending of fact and fiction. Rather than viewing memory as a process of passively retrieving information, folklorist Jeff Titon argues that life stories are actively composed. One anthropologist believes that people author their own lives, much like a novelist writes a book. This literary approach toward autobiography is also echoed by folklorist Sandra Dolby-Stahl, who believes that both narratives about everyday events and the life story are part of a cultural repertoire that draws heavily upon familiar literary genre.[37] These plots include the hero's quest, the immigration saga, the family tragedy and the survival tale. The life story and the personal experience narrative includes both the intimate, idiosyncratic experiences that make up our private lives and those events which are communally shared and part of our collective memory.

Personal Narrative

Defined by one scholar as "informal and spontaneous stories growing out of everyday experiences in all types of communities,"[38] the concept of *personal narrative* is relatively new to the mainstream of folklore scholarship. Early studies tended to represent personal narratives as stories of remarkable and unusual events, though recent studies suggest they often relate ordinary experiences.[39] The personal narrative as a genre often uses dramatized dialogue and stock endings to offer advice, alert another to danger, or even seek praise; it provides a safe and indirect means of communicating disapproval without resorting to overt punishment.[40]

From a psychological viewpoint the personal experience narrative carries the teller's personal stamp. In this sense it is an extension of the narrator's identity, a personal badge which encapsulates both individual and collective meanings.[41] It is also used as a coping mechanism through which narrators achieve greater insight into their lives and rehearse new strategies for facing the future. Says Sandra Dolby Stahl:

> Existentially, the narrator not only acts or experiences but thinks about his actions, evaluates them, learns from them and tells the story – not to express values, but to build them, to create them, to remake them, each time he tells his stories.[42]

While folklore scholars like Linda Degh view the personal narrative as the by-product of imagination and life experiences, others view them as performance events. Not merely narrations, such stories are dramatic performances that draw upon linguistic artistry, cultural knowledge and storytelling competence of the narrator.[43] Many social scientists have suggested that our desire to *narrativize* human experience and dramatize the past stems from an effort to reorganize events in meaningful terms.[44]

There is some evidence that suggests that women's speech and stories tend to have certain stylistic markers, and many scholars have noted gender-specific communication strategies.[45] In her study of female support groups, folklorist Susan Kalcik noted that women tend to talk in phrases that trailed off and observed what she called *kernel story*. These unfinished kernel stories, are highly packed narratives which emerge in interaction and invite women to share their own stories or fill in the gaps;[46] such speech patterns are an attempt to create intimacy and encourage inclusive dialogue.[47]

Forays into the Field: "So what are you going to do for us?"

Before turning to the life stories themselves, one last task remains – to explain how this study was done. With the help of Centro Donne, an Italian women's center situated in the St. Michel area of Montreal, Quebec, I began searching for women to interview. Linda Azzuolo, the head coordinator of the center, met me there and provided me with advice and guidance on how best to proceed. The day I went to Centro Donne, she introduced me to a group of women who were attending a French class. At first I was met with suspicion. After I explained the study, one woman raised her voice and asked: "And what are you going to do for us?" Surprised, antagonized and flustered by the symbolic statement of defiance,[48] I answered with the expected academic demeanor, making reference to the lack of research that had been done on my topic. Appealing to the practical mind, I said that documenting these life stories might shed light on the problems women like herself face and aid community service organizations in raising money for programs for immigrants. Upon reflection, this woman's comment made me realize how often, in advancing our own careers, we scholars take the people we work with for granted and fail to consider the impact of our research on the lives of the people we study.

Having survived the initial test, I did a short group interview. Everybody talked at once, tending to confirm the commonly shared experiences. Collectively, they told a narrative of their immigration experience. After the trial run, I tried to collect names of people who were interested in participating. Although there were a few interested parties, one of the younger women set the tone by saying she was too busy and refusing. Following suit the other women declined. Frustrated but not defeated, I went through the same process with another French class. This time, however, I collected names and talked to the women separately; these women were more receptive.

During one of the Centro Donne celebrations I adopted the same strategy for recruiting interested parties. With the assistance of Linda Azzuolo, the respected and familiar insider, my presence became increasingly acceptable.

On another occasion I made an impromptu appearance at one of the women's auxiliaries that was meeting at a church not far from Centro Donne. The woman responsible for the St. Lucie group was Giuseppina Barbuci, a personal acquaintance. As it turned out, it was a good decision and the women were friendly and accommodating.

The nine women interviewed in depth were from different parts of Italy; they emigrated to Montreal at different times. One of the women spent her childhood in France before returning to Italy and finally settling in Montreal. Another lived in Belgium, while a third worked as a live-in maid in Switzerland and Italian cities such as Rome and Milan. The youngest was Filomena Azzuolo, who works in a factory that makes designer clothes; the eldest was Genoveffa Della Zazzera, a retired woman who is a member of a religious sorority called the Sisters of St. Maria (*l'Armata di Santa Maria*). All the women spoke in their native tongue, some borrowing from their diverse dialects.

Most of the interviews were private, although there were instances when others were present. Filomena Azzuolo's husband sat at the table listening attentively, but he seldom said anything. During Francesca Mancini's interview, her friend Rosilda Di Ciocco was present and sometimes facilitated the process of recollection. To capture the flavor and context of the interviews, I recorded observations on the material culture of women's homes, where most of the interviews took place. Interviews with Giuseppina Barbuci and Graziella Di Corpo were held at a quiet room at Centro Donne. All the women were photographed by Paul J. Perry.

The interviews were informal and open-ended, guided by a series of improvised questions to stimulate conversation. Once the interviews were taped, translated and transcribed, the most salient parts were selected and incorporated into the final work. For readability, the interviews were summarized chronologically, and an attempt was made to preserve the personality and uniqueness of the telling. The lengthier stories, personal experience narratives and other related material are included in the appendix. In places where I felt it most fitting, I inserted personal reactions, commenting on special incidents such as interruptions by neighbors and my own observations.

The fieldwork for this study took place in November and December of 1988. Phase One of the study established the groundwork for the research; in this preliminary stage, I tested questions and responses and refined my research problem. Phase Two involved a continuation of the interviewing through follow-up sessions and new interviews.

For the most part, the interviews went well. At first, some of the women I spoke with were reticent, while some, like Genoveffa Della Zazzera, spoke openly and without reservations. One woman was especially hostile at the beginning, which made for a tense and uncomfortable situation; however, as the interview progressed, her voice became softer and her attitude changed. The transformation that had occurred was quite astonishing.

One final note, this study is presented as a window on the varieties of immigrant women's experiences, with particular attention paid to the issue of gender. From a strict sociological viewpoint, the study does not draw upon a representative sample of Italian-Canadian women. However, one of my main goals in this research is to display the merits of qualitative approaches. While quantitative methods often reduce human experience to statistics, qualitative methods can give us insight into the complexities of women's motivations, desires and life experiences. What such approaches lack in breadth, they make up in depth, and, as such, provide a necessary counterpoint to survey-oriented research.

CHAPTER TWO

The Life Stories

> All autobiographic memory is true. It is up to the interpreter to discover in which sense, where, for which purpose.
>
> Luisa Passerini

Stefania Annibale

> "Eight hours at work, eight hours at home."

Born in 1939 in Agrigento, Sicily, Stefania Annibale is the youngest of four children.[1] She is forty-nine years old, has two daughters and two sons, and is recently widowed. Grieving the loss of her husband, she feels that she has been cheated from enjoying what could have been one of the best times of their life. As a single mother she talks about the emotional and financial difficulties of supporting a family alone. Describing how she and her husband sacrificed much for the the well being of their family, Stefania says: "Well, satisfaction I didn't have much because, eh first the children were small so I waited to take a trip. When they get big . . . " I used to say to myself. "And we never went. We hardly ever went out; we had a family. We couldn't afford it, so now my husband's dead, where am I to go now. Even if I wanted to go to Italy, what will I do there all by myself? Nothing. You can't enjoy yourself without company: everything is different."

Early on in life, she had a great deal of responsibility; she was always busy caring for others. While her brother went to the countryside to work, she stayed home, prepared meals for her sick mother, cleaned and sewed clothes. Because school interfered with her household duties, she only had the chance to complete the third grade. Stefania was nine years old when her mother died; three months later her father died, too. After the death of her parents she and her brother went to live with their grandmother who was a strict disciplinarian and firm believer in the virtues of domesticity.

For entertainment Stefania remembers going to church and meeting with other women friends to embroider, exchange news and talk. To pass the time they would often tell stories or play cards. At sixteen she married and found herself liking married life because it afforded her more freedom. At nineteen she had her first child, Giuseppe; two years later she had her second child, Liborio, followed by her daughters, Maria and Assunta. She stayed home and cared for the children while her husband went to work, taking on jobs in France and Germany.

In 1964, when Stefania was twenty-six, she and her family emigrated to Canada. When they arrived, her husband went to work for Canada Copper Refinery and she went to work in a factory on Chabanel Street, where she made bathing suits.

While she enjoyed working with other Italian women, she also discusses the problem of the double work load that working mothers face on a day-to-day basis: "We were all Italians; the boss was French. The big bosses were Jewish, but they were hardly there. It was a nice factory but then it closed. Then I came home, made supper – you know the same old story: clean, wash clothes, eight hours at home, eight hours at work. I was tired."

Hating the gossiping, nosey neighbors of her village, she likes the privacy and anonymity of the big city. "Here people go to work and mind their own business." Ever since she could remember she always fantasized about leaving her village. To this day she has no desire to return. "I didn't like it, no, no, never. I've been here twenty five years and I've never had any desire to go back to Italy. Never."

Stefania has no regrets about coming to Canada. "When I got here, it seemed that I had lived here for years. I liked it. We found a nice climate, everybody told us you'll see Montreal is cold." However, she conceded there are difficulties. "But we work hard, it's exhausting."

For the time being Stefania hopes the best for her children: "I hope that my children get married, settle down (*sistemati*). I'd be happier, more tranquil, if everyone would be in their own home."

People's homes are emblematic of who they are. They provide glimpses, albeit impressionistic ones, into the lives of the people who inhabit and create them. From the perspective of folklore, they provide scholars with another frame of reference for understanding and knowing the people we study. It is for this reason that I include descriptions of people's intimate surroundings.

After offering me espresso coffee, a piece of cake, and a glass of liquor, we begin the interview. In the basement of her duplex, we sit at the kitchen table. The basement of the Italian immigrant home in some ways has become associated with the place in which the everyday activities of eating, cooking, television viewing and clothes washing occur. The upstairs is reserved for guests and special occasions. This also reduces the maintenance of the household. Except for a few decorative things, the furniture that occupies the basement is plain and functional; it is for everyday use. The upstairs dining room and parlor are adorned with more expensive decorations. The bedrooms are also upstairs.

Although Stefania is reticent at the beginning of the interview, she starts to open up as the interview progresses. However, at no point does she feel comfortable talking about her personal life. Her life seems to have been characterized by having many responsibilities at a young age with elements of self-sacrifice and strong feelings of loyalty toward her family. Summing up what she sees as the essence of her life, she says: "Life was work and home." Stefania's life seems to cover three distinct stages: being a respectable young woman, fulfilling her duties as housewife and mother, and keeping family honor by making sure her daughters are taken care of by marriage. In short, these three phases convey the sex role expectations of Italian traditional culture.

While Stefania has complied with the social mores of her generation, she expresses the strain and pressures that this mentality has placed on her. A strong undercurrent in her personal narratives suggests that, after a long career of service and dedication to husband and children, she deserves to retire. "Now I'm alone, I'm the one who has to think about the home, the money, the children – to work. Everything is up to me . . . too much responsibility. It's hard to keep up with all the work that needs to get done sometimes."

Work has occupied a great deal of Stefania's physical and mental energy. Today she is starting to show the strain of years of conformity to traditional Italian society's ideal of womanhood. In trying to transplant and sustain Old World values in the New World, and lacking the social network and belief system that made those goals desirable and feasible, Stefania finds herself increasingly torn between old cultural values and new social realities.

Filomena Azzuolo

> "I felt the need to go to work."

Filomena Azzuolo is forty-three years old and has one daughter and twin sons. Born in Poffi, in the province of Frosinone, she came to Canada in her early teens. After being a housewife for several years she has returned to working in a factory. Her husband is a bus driver for the city of Montreal. They have been married for over twenty-five years.

While growing up, Filomena lived in an extended family. Her parents, grandparents, brothers and sisters, as well as one married brother, all lived together. Her parents, along with hired help, farmed the land. As for her chores, she helped out with the housework, fed the chickens and sometimes took care of the livestock. Memories of her mother mostly involve her doing housework and preparing meals for the family and laborers. The only time Filomena's mother had time to spend with her children was in the evening at the kitchen table after supper. Filomena recalls how busy and devoted her mother was. "She had very little time to give to us . . . she was always working too much."

Even though Filomena's parents were not wealthy landowners, she admits that they never went without. "We were fine. We didn't need anything; clothes, food wasn't like today, but we had everything that we needed." In the hope of dissuading his children from going into farming, Filomena's father would say: "It's hard work and one doesn't reap much."

As the youngest of the family, Filomena remembers how her older brothers and sisters thought she was the spoiled one. However, as a child, she failed to see her flaws. She says laughingly, "I didn't see my flaws. I was good." When Filomena was young, she and her older brother were very close. When he got older he studied outside the village, and so she only saw him occasionally. But when he came to visit he showered her with gifts and attention.

Paying tribute to one of her favorite relatives, Filomena fondly remembers the game that she and aunt (*zia*) Giovanna played together when she, zia Giovanna, dropped by. Her aunt rewarded her for the special effort. "She was a woman of modest means, so she would say: 'Come, come, Filome, I'll give you the bread from the crow (*cornacchia*).' It wasn't anything special; it was simply bread. I would say: 'No, *zia* Giovannina. I don't want the bread of the *cornacchia*. But if you put an egg in the middle I'll take it or else I won't take the bread; it's like mama's bread [*laughter*].' "

The significant and haunting childhood memories for Filomena are her mother's scary stories of the dangerous forces that lurk in the outside world. As a young child, she remembers how her mother warned her to come home from school as quickly as possible. She repeats the often heard phrase: "Come home quickly, come home quickly[2]. . . don't pay attention to anyone, be careful because there are people who take children away.' This left a mark on my mind, and I was very scared when I had to walk to school . . . we were always in a hurry to get back home from school."

When it came to discussing America, Filomena wondered how life would be in the new land. "I used to think, 'Who knows how America will be? Maybe I can have many clothes, things that I don't have here in Italy. What will it be like to live in a big city?' "

Though Filomena felt sad about leaving her friends behind, she was eager to embark upon her new journey overseas. After some coaxing from their older daughter and son who were already in Canada, Filomena's parents decided to join them. Her parents had more difficulty adjusting to the move. "They had spent half of their life there, and they had laborers whom they ordered around. My parents had never been ordered around before." Filomena talks about a big supper they had with relatives and friends on the day of their departure. "They were all sad that we were leaving."

Filomena had a terrible impression of Canada. "We docked in Halifax. We didn't understand the language. We went to do some grocery shopping but we didn't know any of the products. There were immigrant women with two or three kids in their arms who were crying; those are the women you should interview. When they passed the customs, they threw everything on the floor – suitcases, whatever they were carrying: it was a terrible feeling."

The train ride to Montreal proved to be disappointing. "We took the train across a forest. Every once in a while there was a small house and I would say this is not America; let's go back home."

In Italy Filomena had completed the fifth grade in elementary school; however, when she started school in Canada, they placed her a year behind. She explains the circumstances that led her to quit school and go to work. "School was awful; I didn't understand anything. I felt ashamed that they put me a year behind – fourth grade. I was fourteen years old. One day I fell and broke my leg and so I never went back to school. I had lost a year of school and didn't want to go back. My brother tried to encourage me by telling me: 'Don't feel ashamed, school is important, it's good.' But I didn't want go back."

At fifteen, Filomena found a job in a factory where her mother worked. There is a smile on Filomena's face when she remembers how she and her cousin tried to make the boring job of cutting thread into a pleasant experience, "We would organize ourselves in such a way that the day would go by fast, try to make the best of it." Once she started to work, she continued because her earnings helped with family expenses. At eighteen, Filomena married one of her brother's friends. They were neighbors and worked close by. "In those days people didn't date; they married." She made it very clear that nobody had forced the marriage upon them; it was their choice. Shortly after she gave birth to Linda, twin sons followed. At that time Filomena concentrated her efforts on motherhood. Since the twins were born prematurely and prone to illness, she stayed home to make sure that they were progressing smoothly with their physical development. Although she expresses ambivalent feelings about staying at home to care for her children, she feels that it was her obligation. "My responsibility was to the children, first."

Once her children were grown she returned to work. Feeling bored, dissatisfied and anxious, Filomena became lonely and desired the company of others. "After the kids were a little more grown up I was fed up with staying home. I felt that I

wanted to go out, see people. I had become nervous
and agitated . . . so I went back to the factory. I
thought I might be able to help the family differ-
ently. I felt the need to go out for them; maybe one
day they might want to go to school. I would help
my husband along."

In this context, the factory was not only a press-
ing economic necessity but also a personal choice
that held psychological benefits. Today, what would
bring Filomena great pleasure is to see her children
settle down (*sistemati*). She feels once they settle,
her life will be complete and free of worries. In her
old age Filomena hopes to take a trip to a place with
a warm climate where she could find some relief for
the ailments that she expects to develop over the
years. She is optimistic: "I got from life more than I
expected."

As for her attitude toward Italy, she feels
detached and un-nostalgic toward her birth place.
Canada is her home, where her family and most of
her relatives live.

I met Filomena in her home in St. Leonard, a sub-
urb of Montreal where many Italians have settled,
and where one finds many Italian pastry shops, bars
and grocery stores, along with banks where Italian
is spoken. In fact, it is not unusual to see signs up in
the windows of some of the shopkeepers that read:
Qui si parla italiano (Here we speak Italian).

The youngest of the women I interviewed,
Filomena is a tall, forty-three-year-old woman with

curly brown hair. When I arrived, she and her husband gave me a friendly greeting and led me into the kitchen. Her husband was present at the interview. He was interested and curious about my studies, and I felt it inappropriate to ask him to leave. When they found out that I study in the United States, Filomena asked me how my mother coped with the situation and immediately empathized with her "predicament." That very same evening she expected her son, who was studying in Ontario, to come to visit for the holidays. She told me that she found it difficult to accept her son's going away to study, although now she is becoming more used to it.

As is the custom, she asked me if I cared for something to eat and offered me cookies. Like the other Italian homes I had been in, the kitchen floors were covered with ceramic tiles and had been decorated with what looked like a Spanish-style dining room set.

One of the clearest themes to emerge from the interview was Filomena's strong identification with the mother role. She appeared to have channeled a great deal of her energy into raising her children and placing the family's needs first. A case in point was her decision to go back to work. Though her choice was a conscious effort to break away from her feelings of isolation, part of her reason for returning to work was her family. The apparent rationalization was that the extra money generated from work offered more possibilities for her children, especially with regard to their education. Since the needs of the family in Italian traditional culture are considered primary, justification of a decision based on personal choice should include some advantages for the welfare of the group; otherwise it might be frowned upon by the community. For Filomena going to work made her more self-assured. As a result her knowledge of the French language has improved and she can speak a little English.

While Filomena would have preferred to have had the opportunity to train for a better occupation, she has no regrets about her life. Stating the common Italian immigrant hope for upward mobility, Filomena says: "What I didn't do, maybe my children will do." Here, a sense of accomplishment is vicariously experienced through the achievements of the next generation. The dislocating effects of the immigration experience are given meaning. It is the hope of the parents to turn a life of denial and self-sacrifice into a purposeful investment in the future of their children.

Another important theme in almost all the interviews was the fear fostered by repeated parental warnings that bogeymen and other vaguely defined evils lurked outside the home. These stories instilled such fear in Filomena as a child that she was afraid to walk back from school. Part of the power of these incomplete narratives stems from their ambiguity. The imagination of a young child can be far more frightening than any specific threat the teller might have elaborated.

In the entertaining story of "*zia Giovannanina's cornacchia*," Filomena paid special tribute to one of her favorite aunts. One senses that engaging in this playful exchange was *zia* Giovanna's way of sharing with her a gift. Since she could not offer the young Filomena any material gifts, she redefined the situation by creatively devising a meaningful activity. In sharing this moment with me, Filomena continued her aunt's tradition.

Giuseppina Barbuci

> "So I was always strong, always!"

Giuseppina Barbuci was born in the Abruzzo region of Italy in the town of Santo. She is married, has two sons and has lived in Montreal since 1957. At fifty-eight she is an active member of Centro Donne and is the head of a woman's church auxiliary. We conducted the interview in one of the small offices at Centro Donne.

Giuseppina describes her parents as hard-working peasants who lived in the countryside away from the center of town. While she remembers the hardships that certain families experienced, she does not recall ever going without. "There were families that suffered. We suffered from fear of the war but we didn't need anything." Her mother walked daily to the well to get fresh water because they did not have running water. Her mother had to go for water, with the bucket (*conca*) on her head, one child in her arms and another holding on to her skirt. She comments on the hard life her mother had while raising seven children: "I don't know how she did it. If I were to do what she did I don't think I could do it." After a difficult childbirth, Giuseppina's mother was hospitalized for three months. At that time her aunt removed Giuseppina from grade school because she felt there were things to take care of at home. Although today Giuseppina finds herself with little formal schooling, she does not feel bitter toward her parents. "I feel bad, but I can't say that I can blame my parents; it wasn't their fault."

As a young woman, she remembers going with her mother and sisters to pick olives and thresh wheat. The women of her family usually went along with the laborers; to the young Giuseppina, the whole event was a festive occasion, where fun and entertainment were mixed with work. "There were always ten or fifteen of us, and there we sang, joked. It was nice, I liked it; it was out in the open."

One of her favorite pastimes was working on the tractor. When the season changed and spring came, she spent time tanning on the balcony with three or four friends. These were times when talk of boyfriends, family matters and gossip was exchanged.

When Giuseppina came to Canada, she had been engaged for three years. She says mockingly, "I came as a free person, in this land of freedom." Although she tried to sponsor her fiancé's trip to join her in Canada, he could not leave; he had been unfairly labeled a Communist by the Italian authorities. Though it was a difficult decision to make, Giuseppina decided to stay in Canada with her family. During this time she thought of all the girlfriends she knew in Italy who had been abandoned by suitors who left for Switzerland or Germany. A few years later she married a young man from her new neighborhood.

In discussing the numerous suitors she had in Italy she points out what she considers to be qualities of good candidates for marriage: Men with good manners and who promised to be good providers made for good husbands. Knowing the family of the man is always a good guarantee of his moral character and his economic status within the community. "My husband – he is poor and honorable."

Good manners, above all, was especially important to Giuseppina when she was considering suitors for marriage: "You know, I liked a boy who held the door, held your hand, all these things; even if he was abrasive in other areas, as long as he had these qualities."

Her first impressions of Canada were disappointing. She has vivid memories of docking in Halifax. "To see those poor Italians with their suitcases . . . I was very disappointed with the customs in Halifax. I was like the Italian immigrants, but I was watching them not me. All that stuff people brought, like cured ham, *prosciutto*, sausages, was confiscated. I saw trunks being emptied, and this truly disturbed me."

She also expected America to be glamorous. She remembers thinking: "Well, Madonna when I go there, you know, America! You know how it is and now I'm used to it."

A year before leaving for Canada, in a dream,

Giuseppina had a eerily accurate vision of her future place of employment. "The factory where I went to work, I dreamed about it, the same, same, you see [*raising her arm to show me*] and up here there were rows of threads, already cut and they were placed in cartons, all colors. I had dreamed of this rack of threads exactly like this one [*the rack at the factory*], the same, same, right before coming here, one year before."

Four days after Giuseppina arrived in Canada she started working in a men's suit factory. Though she found it difficult to do piece work and staying seated for eight hours straight, she liked the company of other women. "We were always in good spirits (*allegre*); we used to sing, joke." It was there that she learned the various Italian dialects. Jokingly she says: "I learned Campobassano, Calabrese, Sicilian, Abruzzese – all types of Italian. I learned a word from each, except English or French." In 1972, she stopped working to take care of her aging parents who lived in the apartment above hers. Her husband thought it was foolish to give more tax money to the government just because we were earning two incomes, so Giuseppina quit her job. Today she regrets this decision, because her pension is smaller than it could have been.

Giuseppina's parents always lived close by – sometimes in the same apartment block, sometimes on the same floor with an adjoining door. When Giuseppina left for work in the morning her mother would look after the children. The extended family network facilitated Giuseppina's work outside the home, and she recognizes the valuable service her mother provided. "She raised my children and my sister's children."

Today Giuseppina spends her time as a community organizer, planning events and activities for the women's church auxiliary group of St. Lucie. At Centro Donne she coordinates the coffee hour, called Café Rencontre, where professionals and special guests come to talk about health care, planned parenthood and other subjects. With regard to her community work, she feels she has gained a great deal from interacting with other people. "If I had stayed at home," she says, "I wouldn't have known what I know." In this respect she is also grateful for her husband's cooperation.

She reflects upon the problems involved with getting Italian women to participate in community activities. "There are three categories of women [who don't participate]: those who think people will criticize them, those who think they can't spare the time (but I think if one wants to find the time it can be found), and those whose husbands forbid them." As for the future generation, she feels, while they have advanced themselves in terms of education, some are worse off than earlier immigrants because of the drugs and apathy.

She expresses gratitude toward her husband. "We understand each other. He isn't jealous. He never counted my money. He gives me his money; I go to the bank . . . I do what I want; I respect him." In keeping with her independent personality, she says, "I think that if I had a husband who watched my every move I think I might have either left him or [*makes a hand gesture that represents horns by extending her index and pinky and curling her thumb over the two fingers*] cuckolded him (*gli avrei messo le corne*). . . eh, if you don't have a choice."

Throughout Giuseppina's personal narrative are suspenseful wartime stories. One story tells of a near brush with death when the Germans came with machine guns searching for men. Another relates the time when her family harbored nine Canadian soldiers (see *Appendix*, Barbuci, "The Germans," "Nine Canadian Soldiers").[3] She remembers how funny it was to watch the Canadian soldiers eat spaghetti. In one instance, she describes her philosophy of choosing a mate (see *Appendix*, Barbuci, "Suitors"). A strong willed woman with a clear sense of self and identity emerges. She speaks of how she stayed away from one of her suitors because he mistreated his mother. Her reasoning is that if he verbally abused his mother in public, how would he treat his own wife?

Giuseppina becomes a character in the stories that she creates, by casting herself as the feisty peasant who exercises wiliness (*furberia*) in everything that she does. Once she taught the rich, cocky boy of the area a lesson by giving him a swollen knee. Or again she took pride in her modest background by socializing with "average families" (see *Appendix*, Barbuci, "Average Families").

Giuseppina's own character in the stories is always ready to offset her opponent with a quick, witty remark. This style of speech is similar to the verbal bantering Richard Gambino noted among southern Italian women in his book *Blood of My Blood*. Verbal skills were found to be especially important in a bargaining situation, which gives the client negotiating power.[4] Sociologist Herbert Gans recorded similar observations in his research, in which he found that women had greater verbal proficiency than men.[5] Folklorist Roger Abrahams' study of black women's conversational styles also reveals how this type of image, conveyed through the spoken word, is a means of making a public statement and negotiating meanings with others, especially in interaction with the opposite sex.[6] In this style of speech, Giuseppina appears to have found a strategy by which she can turn her second-class gender status into a position of privilege.

By redefining limitations to suit personal and social needs, Giuseppina appears to have designed a character strong enough to overcome any challenge. The series of stories revolving around the subject of suitors and relationships are a living expression of Giuseppina's persona in action (see *Appendix*, Barbuci, "Suitors," "Average Families" and "Community Work"). In retelling them, she reasserts her autonomy and free will.

As the flip side of the nurturing, self-denying mamma that we often see in movies, Giuseppina is ready to defend her rights. Her narrative projects an exaggerated image of strength. Engaging in parody and a rhetorical game of power and control, Giuseppina conveys an over-blown picture of her ideal self as a mythical warrior ready to avenge any wrongdoing. Such stories as "*Le corne*" (see *Appendix,* Barbuci, "The Horns") demonstrate this process in action. It expresses her belief in personal freedom and choice. Her reflections on the community further reinforce this crafted image.

As some of the women in this study have shown, the factory experience is not entirely negative or detrimental. For Giuseppina, work is a positive experience that offers a place for joking and an atmosphere of joy (*allegria*). Like many of the women, she too enjoys participating in obscene bantering and bawdy joke telling at the factory (see *Appendix*, Barbuci, "Joke").

Antonietta De Fronzo

Born in the tourist town of Giovinazzo, Bari, Antonietta De Fronzo is from a family of nine children. This fifty-four-year-old widow has four children. With the small pension she receives from the government and the help of her children she manages to make ends meet.

While working for a gas company in New York City, her father was in an accident that damaged his eye sight. At that time he was an illegal alien and not eligible for workman's compensation. Antonietta jokingly said that, when he returned to Italy, he kept himself busy by fathering more children. Even though life was hard, their family managed with her mother's sewing, her father's carpentry work and the pension they received. Her parents died shortly after her departure for Canada in 1965.

Antonietta went to school up to fifth grade and then attended sewing school (*scuola di taglio*). She did a bit of everything – embroidery, knitting and lacemaking (*l'ucinetto*). Her other social activities included spending time with female friends and, making excuses so that she and her friends could go for walks in the square (*piazza*) and watch the boys. Storytelling was a favorite pastime as well. She would huddle around the brazier (*braciere*) with her mother who told children's rhymes and frightening bedtime stories of young children being kidnapped.

Although she had aspirations of becoming a hairdresser, Antonietta never had the opportunity to pursue this interest. As a young woman, she did not want to marry a "man of agriculture, of the country." Her father had been what she called an "industrialist," and she aspired for something more. From the outset she was fond of her husband. He was to my liking (*mi era venuto in simpatia*). "He was cheerful (*allegro*)." After eight months of courtship they married. She was twenty-four years old.

Before coming to Canada, Antonietta knew what America was like. "My sister-in-law sent us a postcard with women in suits and fancy hats. In Italy people weren't doing so well, we lived modest lives." Even though her husband had a good job he insisted that they leave. When they arrived in Canada with their two children, Pietro and Franco, no one liked it here. However, because of the lack of money and the debts from the trip, they could not go back to Italy.

Since her husband had been having difficulty finding work, Antonietta went to work in a factory on Chabanel Street, one of the oldest textile districts in Montreal. At work she experienced guilt and conflict about leaving her children with other people. Her socialization in Italy did not prepare her for the role of the working mother. "In Italy the women didn't work outside the home." Although she enjoyed the company of other Italian women at the factory, she finally left her job because she worried about the welfare of her children. Her husband worked for a while, training as an apprentice placing tiles, but after a series of medical problems he had to stop work altogether.

For the time being, Antonietta lives in an apartment with her daughter and son. She is grateful to them for the emotional and financial support they have provided her. Her children have not "abandoned" her by making her live elsewhere. "I have nothing to complain about, but, see, others have children who get to be a certain age and they leave home. Me, my children, they didn't do that, they married; they call me, visit, they don't leave me alone."

Before starting the interview Antonietta offers me something to drink. As I drink a glass of mineral water and set up the tape recorder, she asks me questions about my studies. Her home has the ceramic floor tiles commonly found in Italy. Her kitchen is simple and functional and not as ornate as some of the other homes I had visited. This might reflect her economic situation or her personal taste.

Midway into the interview Antonietta starts to show me her family albums with photos of her relatives and children and her home town of Giovinazzo. She is very proud of her family and describes the events associated with each picture. She also has a souvenir family photograph of her cruise ship voyage to Canada.

With her husband dead, Antonietta gains a great sense of satisfaction from her children and is especially partial toward her daughter. After having three boys she was glad to have a girl, and when she shows off her daughter's picture she refers to her as her queen.

Antonietta expresses a fatalistic attitude throughout her narrative. Canada did not live up to her expectations. Her recollections of life in Italy are more positive and idyllic. She nostalgically looks at the past: "Back then there was respect. I don't know, people here are not as warm as people in Italy."

She misses the kinship networks that were available in her home town. Also, sharing living arrangements with her sister-in-law did not prove to be a good experience. The tension and strife of this situation aggravates her misgivings about having moved to Canada in the first place.

Antonietta feels distraught by the apparent economic and emotional distance between her family and her relatives. She feels betrayed by what she perceives to be the corrupting influence of money. "Now people have money. I don't know, the rich are not sincere. The rich keep you under their feet. There's my brother and my sister-in-law, they're better off then I am, and they never come here; they never come to visit me."

Although a somber mood hangs over most of the interview, Antonietta is most animated when recalling children's rhymes and stories from her childhood. This appears to be one of the happiest periods in her life. She takes great pleasure in acting out the children's rhymes of precocious birds and talking clocks. The story of "The Chestnut" (see *Appendix*, De Fronzo, "Il cecce") instills fear in the hearts of children, they go to bed promptly and more easily conform to the rules of the adult world. The children's rhymes and stories are performed playfully and without sorrow or regret. While singing them, Antonietta seems to be living the experience all over again. It is difficult to convey the richness and intensity of the moment. In listening, I couldn't help but think about the liberating value of such folkloric recreations for the listener, as well as the performer. There is something magical about them indeed.

Anna Del Negro

Anna Del Negro is a sixty-year-old retired seamstress who was born in Carpineto Sinello in the Abruzzo region of Italy. The youngest of seven children, she has lived in Canada for the last thirty-two years. Before coming to Canada she lived in Belgium, where her husband worked as a miner. She has three children, Osvaldo, Luciano and myself, and a granddaughter named Tanya.

With the hope of improving their situation, Anna's parents moved from Carpineto Sinello to the bigger nearby town of Gissi. Anna's father was a butcher and merchant (*commerciante*). He walked to the county fairs in the neighboring villages to buy livestock so that he could have fresh meat for the butcher shop. "We lived thanks to the butcher shop; my father bought goats (*capretti*) and pigs. He was a *commerciante*; we also used to sell eggs, salami, cheese, a little bit of everything. We used to get up at five o'clock in the morning to prepare the fresh meat at the butcher shop." After a long day's work, they would eat at noon and then sleep till 4:00, resting from the day's activities.

When Anna was ten years old, her mother died from gall bladder stones. As her illness grew worse, her mother took the time to explain to her about menstruation, warn her of boys and stress the importance of being chaste before marriage. Along with providing her with important advice on womanhood, Anna's mother left her a dowry (*dote*) stocked with special linens, towels, hand-laced tablecloths and other things that a newlywed might need to start her life as a homemaker.

Breakfast at the Di Paolo household was a memorable event. In the morning Lucia, Anna's mother, would boil a big pot of milk and coffee (*caffèlatte*), which was made from barley (*orzo*). "We would dunk our bread and we ate like little sheep." As it was the practice among the self-employed men (*negozianti*) of the region, Anna's father went to the bar for coffee. Recalling this ritual she said, "He wasn't a man of the house. He was a *negoziante*. He had money, not a lot, but enough for his family, independence, so he went to the bar."

From her early childhood years, Anna played games like hide and seek (*topatopa*) and a stick and ball game (*curso*) and acted as goalie in the neighborhood games of soccer (*pallone*). For the most part, these games were only played among girls. "My mother scolded me for coming home with bruised knees."

At the Christmas holidays, Anna eagerly awaited the gifts that the old hag (*la befana* – the legendary old lady that comes by on Christmas) would bring on January 6, the Epiphany. During this time of the year people gave oranges, hard nougat candy (*torrone*) and chocolates. "*La befana*, she's like *Bewitched* the TV program, a witch that brings children gifts." In Belgium there was St. Nicholas (*San Nicola*). She sings:

Oh grand San Nicola, patron des écoliers,
apportez-moi beaucoup . . . de souliers . . .
beaucoup de jouets.

(Oh great St. Nicholas, caretaker of school children.
Bring me lots . . . of shoes . . .
lots of toys.)

One of her favorite pastimes was going to the movies. A fan of Italian cinema, her father used to hide her underneath his cape and sneak her in to watch popular Italian movies. Such films included *Il lupo della montagna* (The Wolf of the Mountain), *La cieca di Sorrento* (Blindwoman of Sorrento), *Figli di nessuno* (Nobody's Children) and *La mamma che ritorna* (The Mother Who Returns), with such popular Italian actors as Amedeo Nazzare, Massimo Girotto and Fausto Giachetti.

As Anna got older, the church became the meeting place where young women went to see and be seen by potential suitors. At a distance, unmarried women and men gazed at each other, communicating with glances and gestures. In this public sphere such types of courting rituals were acceptable. "Once in a while there were young boys who placed themselves behind columns and made eyes at you. That's the courting we did (*l'amore che facevamo*, which literally means the love that we made in courtship). We used to go to church to see young boys." They also went for long walks under the pine trees along a special path in Gissi; here too young people would exchange a smile or a look.

Anna remembers a courtship ritual from a slightly earlier period. With her first sister, Anna recalled how suitors came at two or three o'clock in the morning to sing and play violin. If they came early, people would throw water at them to chase them away. "They sang love songs. They wrote poems among themselves and recited them."

Village songs were also sung as a means of voicing community disapproval or harming a person's reputation by casting doubt on his/her moral character. It also was a means of taking revenge. One such song involved a young woman named Nannin who, upon her mother's advice, declined a marriage proposal. "I remember once a girl was very much in love with a young man; and then her mother didn't want her to marry this man. Her name was Naninn, like me, and they sang a song about her. It was a scandal around town." This was a song of sexual transgression and betrayal. Anna sang a few verses:

> E a bal pa' San Giovanni ce sem incontrata,
> la gente ha detto che tu eri una sfacciata.
> E sopra la poltrona se sagiata qualcosa de buona
> e mo te ne pu scorda.

> (Down by San Giovanni we met.
> People said that you were shameless,
> And on top of the couch you tasted something good
> That you can't forget.)

Although Anna did not describe her father as strict, she did think that her brothers had more freedom. The cultural mores of the time dictated that the women's domain was the home while the world of affairs and politics belonged to men. "My father loved us all – it's only that I was a girl and things were different. Men could go out more often; they could go out. I had to stay home. My sister cooked. I did the dishes, swept the floor, dried the utensils."

Because there was a lack of money to send all seven children to school, the girls in the family were sent to learn a trade (*mestiere*), while the older boys enjoyed a few extra years of schooling. From the ages of fourteen to seventeen Anna worked as an apprentice seamstress.

When Anna turned eighteen, her father decided it was time that she married. Even though she wanted to wait until she was older, her father thought otherwise. Relatives told Anna that her sister Irisa had impersonated her at a legal wedding ceremony at city hall and signed her name in the marriage register; later, Anna was pressured into a formal church wedding. When it was time to choose furniture, her sister once again denied her a voice by deciding for her.

In listening to Anna describe this event, I could hear her grapple, on the one hand, with her feelings of love and loyalty toward her family and, on the other hand, with her contempt for those same people who forced her into an arranged marriage. "My father was very nice and everything, but for me this was something that will always be a sore point in my heart." There were other places in Anna's personal experience narrative where her older sister Irisa played the role of the domineering, substitute mother. Although Anna did not outwardly condemn her sister, she clearly resents her involvement in her personal affairs.

Although Anna was married, two years of dating passed before she and her husband Giovanni actually lived together. "There was an eight-day reception – pastries, jordon almonds. People came from Carpineto, Furci, Gissi and then I went to San Buono, my father's village."

Soon after their first child, Anna's husband Gio-

vanni left for Belgium to work as a miner. At the
time Belgium and Italy had an agreement: Belgium
sent coal to Italy in exchange for cheap labor. Many
Italians died from work-related diseases such as
black lung (*fibrosa*). The mining disaster of 1949
took the lives of forty-seven Italian miners in Trazeg-
nie, Belgium; twenty-nine of those were from the
same Italian town, Lama dei Peligni. Giovanni, my
father, was one of three survivors and was awarded
a medal of bravery from the Belgian government for
risking his life to save two of his fellow workers.
"The Italian government sold its people and they
were victims of an awful disease called *fibrosa* . . . so
many of my husband's friends – the same thing; he
escaped death because he came to Canada. Otherwise he would have met the same fate."

Two years later Anna joined her husband in Belgium. In 1951 she had her second child, Luciano.
Proudly describing the birth she said, "I had a natural labor with a midwife – no doctor. The labor was
normal; of course you don't bear a child without
any pain. It always hurts."

Anna found life in Belgium pleasant. One of the
most difficult things was learning the language, but
her neighbor, Mariette Ferdinand Du Pont, offered
assistance. "We were very happy there; we made an
error to come to Canada. Life was much harder here;
we spoke the language, but the climate was cold."
While most of the miners lived in shacks that had
been built for prisoners during the war, Anna and her
family were fortunate to find suitable housing.

Because of deteriorating health, Anna's husband

Giovanni immigrated to Canada to look for work. When he first left, he went to Ontario where he, along with relatives and others from the village, worked on the railroad tracks. By the time he went to Quebec he had worked in Windsor and Toronto. Two years later, Anna and her children joined her husband in Montreal. When Anna arrived in 1957, her husband worked as a presser at the Jocardi coat factory; she started working in the same factory. Though the job was tiring, she joked with other Italian immigrant women. Amongst themselves they talked about what they had prepared for supper the night before and sometimes poked fun at the sexual demands of their spouses.

In 1961 I was born. At that time she and my father owned a small grocery store called Giovanni Fruit Store. The store catered largely to an Italian clientele, selling Italian products that could not be found in the Canadian supermarkets. Osvaldo, the eldest son, helped with the business, working behind the butcher counter and making deliveries. Other family members briefly found employment there. Since the store was located in the same building in which we lived, there was always someone running down the stairs to transmit a message or up the stairs for a hot meal and coffee. There was always a great deal of activity, especially since my aunts and uncles all lived in the same apartment building. Child care was based on a close network of kinship and mutual aid.

Next to the grocery was the Montrose Cinema (later called Le Septième Art; it currently is a recreational center). Inside the apartment building was a small courtyard where the children played dodge-ball games. Through the courtyard we would sneak into the cinema's back door to see Dracula movies, westerns and a mixture of French and American B-movies. The courtyard was also a place where women exchanged news and gossip as they hung out wet clothes to dry. To the children, the building was a place for exploring corridors, running up and down stairs and pulling pranks. Although children roamed freely into the homes of close relatives, the unwritten rule was that supper time should not be disturbed by visitors; to do so was considered rude. Some time later Anna and Giovanni sold the gro-cery store, and opened a family-operated restaurant called Da Giovanni. Located in a busy industrial sector of Montreal, the restaurant occupied half of the first floor of its building. French-Canadian and Italian fast food was offered – pea soup, french fries with gravy sauce, oven-baked pizza and spaghetti. Like the grocery store, the restaurant was open seven days a week. Anna worked during the day, while her husband worked the night shift. The old-est son, Osvaldo, worked too, running deliveries, cooking and washing dishes.

After selling the restaurant, Anna and Giovanni bought a convenience store (*Tabagie Variété*) locat-ed in a downtown high-rise apartment building called the Tadoussac. One could buy cigarettes, magazines, newspapers, perfume, imported choco-lates and other goods. Again, Anna often worked the morning shift, while her husband worked late at

night. Because of the numerous holdups and bur-
glaries, Anna and Giovanni finally sold the store.

During this time Anna had built up a home-
operated sewing business in which she did alter-
ations and designed and sewed clothes. She built up
a profitable clientele. Throughout her working
career, Anna used her sewing skills to supplement
the family income. Like other immigrant women,
Anna sometimes worked in the black market, doing
piece work and getting paid under the table. For a
brief time she was the seamstress for a private
designer boutique called Huguette. She then
worked for the Sears department store doing alter-
ations.

Strongly family-oriented, Anna has a certain nostal-
gia for the kinship ties that existed in the Old Country. As she gets older she feels relatives and the
younger generation are growing more distant, less
concerned with nurturing close family ties. Mourn-
ing the loss of loyalty toward the family, she says:
"In this life now we think only of our own. I
remember during our time the family was not only
the children, but aunts and uncles; we were all united. In America everyone has become egotistical;
they have their homes, they have a little money and
they distance themselves from the family. This is
very difficult for me to accept; it's better to have
nothing and have family. It's very important."

Looking back, Anna feels she has been very gen-
erous, always thinking about her family, sending

money to her brothers, sisters and father. For thirty-four years she has been the one to keep a close correspondence with the family, writing letters and cards. Referring to her husband's lack of involvement in these matters she says: "He never wrote a line on a letter, I always wrote; now I am getting old but only a while ago I sent twenty greeting cards. It's important. When Christmas arrives one receives word from a friend or relative, one is pleased."

Reflecting on her marriage, she thinks her husband lived up to his obligations by making sure the family's needs were taken care of. She also feels that he was a good husband inasmuch as he didn't deprive her of money, like some men. "He loves his children too. He is not very demonstrative, but he cares for all of you very much." However, she can never understand his attitude toward her appearance: "He bought me pretty things; he always wanted me to dress well, with costume jewelry, but when I did dress well he was jealous. He's of the old generation."

If Anna were to do it all over again, she says she "would make her own decisions." She would work as she did, because "without work one doesn't reap." "If you want to live a good life, you should not impose your will on others, the way some people have tried to do to me in the past, you must be fair. Now I would be in control, be fair, reasonable, consult with people, love each other. Life brings you nothing but grief if you are too capricious. It's important when people love each other."

As for the future, she hopes that I marry a nice, hard-working, caring young man who isn't jealous.

"I wish to see you happy without having to sacrifice like we have."

The kitchen is the perfect spot for the interview with my mother. It was, and still is, a space that was familiar to us. Although my mother has a separate room where she does her sewing, the kitchen is the place where she cooks, writes letters and cheques, makes phone calls and receives visitors and relaxes. Her kitchen, like the ones in many of the other women's homes, has ceramic tiles on the floor. It is divided by a small counter three-fourths of the width of the room which has a glass case at the top and the bottom. Inside are special cups, family heir-looms and glassware. On top of the counter is where the phone sits, along with phone books, pieces of paper and a collection of pencil holders that seldom have pens that work. The glass that covers part of the credenza is adorned with a small floral design. In one corner there are photographs of nieces and relatives and a pocket size picture of the Virgin Mary.

All the kitchenware is on one side of the room, along with the red refrigerator, matching stove, dishwasher and other appliances. The other side is for dining. On the side of the credenza are two pantries. In the middle there is a mirror inset into the wall with several small shelves running along it. On each shelf there are wedding favors such as candy-coated almonds (*confetti*) wrapped in gauze, and souvenirs with pictures of Santa Cabrini. On the wall next to the pantries are calendars with cop-per objects from Italy and photographs of other saints. In front of the kitchen there is an enclosed terrace with a wood furnace and sliding glass doors. On the wall separating those doors hangs a framed photograph of cheese, bread and fruit – symbols of abundance (*abbondanza*).[7] The dining room tends toward Spanish style furniture. The table is covered with a beige lace tablecloth protected by a transparent plastic cover. In the center is usually a crystal vase with colorful artificial flowers. The top parts of the chairs are upholstered with a gold velvet material which is covered with specially made plastic.

Anna's narratives reveals a variety of themes. Her repertoire touches upon every aspect of life – from the supernatural to village life – and it includes songs that celebrate female sexuality. The evocative images, tales and songs Anna relates in her life story embody traditional Italian beliefs and express her unique personality and attitude toward life (see *Appendix*, Del Negro, "Folk Beliefs," "Riverito," "È la fonte di Carpineto").

Her repertoire of supernatural tales contains two about witches (see *Appendix*, Del Negro, "Folk Beliefs"). One story describes the heroic act of a family member in saving a young infant from being sacrificed in a witchcraft ritual: it contains all the elements of drama – conflict, tension and a final resolution. Another narrative deals with witch testing, relating the time my mother's sister-in-law, Cleonica, immobilized a witch by plunging a knife into the table. Fortune-telling events and a folk cure can also be found in my mother's reminiscence, attesting to her belief in the supernatural forces.

Another important theme that emerges from the interviews is the portrayal of village life in Italy as a simpler, more caring time. In this idyllic past the village is devoid of stress and conflict, class distinctions become unimportant and people greet each other regardless of social standing. In praising the benefits of small-town living, Anna subtly expresses her reservations about the fast pace of urban life. The humorous story about the time she was too tired to recite a poem in her elementary class also attests to a period when people were kinder and more compassionate (see *Appendix*, Del Negro, "Community").

The story of how her sewing teacher refused to continue with classes pointedly conveys a meaningful lesson about obeying authority: Anna had not addressed her with the formal greeting "Riverito." More importantly, however, it shows a battle of will between an adolescent and an authority figure.

For Anna, songs congeal memories and feelings from the past. They are her favorite medium of expression. The act of singing brings to life a repertoire of characters, situations and events. In the lamenting song of a young man who has fallen under the spell of the young maiden Marusella, one senses an aesthetic sensibility at play. In her performance, Anna shares a meaning-making activity with the listener. With local songs, like the cheerful rendition of "È la fonte di Carpineto" (The Fountain of Carpineto), she pays homage to her birth place. The rhythmic lullaby "Nell', Nell' " conveys with its upbeat lyrics a similar lighthearted, playful mood. Another lullaby "Dormi, dormi" tends more toward a feeling of despair; it is sung in a hushed tone, with a slow whining sound suggestive of grief or an anticipated loss. In "La bella che piangeva" (The Crying Beauty), Anna describes the sorrow of a young girl whose soldier boyfriend is killed at war. Here, she pays tribute to her father by singing one of his favorite songs.

When Anna recalls the songs from her past she is instantly transformed into a performer. The kitchen becomes her stage and I am the audience. More importantly, the act of singing is a cathartic experience that provides her with moments of great pleasure. This is her medium.

For my mother, singing is a means of transforming the mundane into something festive and memorable. Songs have the power to transcend reality. As she sings the songs of her village, I hear the echoes of a different time reverberate into the present. Together the words paint the evocative scenery of the village (*paese*); they belong to the type of song village girls might sing doing housework or perhaps going for walks. The cheerful song of "È la fonte di Carpineto" is especially visual, expressing a carefree spirit of walking in the open air.

Genoveffa Della Zazzera

Born in Conca della Campania, originally part of Naples, Genoveffa Della Zazzera is a small silver-haired woman of eighty-five who speaks in a

Neapolitan dialect. She has two married daughters and lives by herself in an apartment where one of her daughters occupies the upper floor. Seeking a better way of life, she emigrated to Canada in 1951, a year after her husband.

Her parents were farmers and strongly religious. As she recalls, even during harvest they would get up at four o'clock in the morning to go to mass. She yearns for what she views as a simpler, more serene life. "There was that joy, it's not like today, one thinks of bad things right away. No, there wasn't that maliciousness, that evil like today, life was more simple." As a young woman, Genoveffa had aspirations of becoming a nun. Her older brother went to Pallotini Seminary in Rome to become a priest and the family thought one member in a religious order was sufficient. She remembers her mother saying, "I have a son who's a priest, there is no need for you to become a nun. You are the last and you have to help us out [*waving her hand at me*]." One thing that stands out in her memory is the earthquake of 1915. With the dramatic fervor of a stage actress, she says, "I was small, I didn't understand, I started to feel the earth shake, my mother started to scream: 'Run away, run away. Earthquake,' my mother screams. The house was far from town. Then the wall in the big room started to crumble, then the staircase."

In 1927 Genoveffa was married. She had her first child in 1930 and her second in 1935. She describes this phase in her life as a turning point. Her husband was involved in "a thousand" trades, and was away for long periods of time, going from town to town selling fruit. "His father [her father-in-law] was a saintly man. He didn't drink, smoke. But he [her husband] liked to drink, smoke and gamble." Her husband appeared to be a strict authoritarian and quick-tempered man. He died of cancer several years ago.

Her first few years in Montreal were hard, especially because of the difference in language. She remembers feeling completely helpless at the grocery store and going to the post office without even knowing how to say "stamp" in French. As for her experience with French Canadians, she says philosophically: "There are good ones and there are bad; some were nice, understanding, others said: *'Maudits italiens, mangez la merde'* (Damn Italians, eat shit)."

Even after living in Canada for almost thirty-four years, Genoveffa feels a strong emotional attachment to Italy, while acknowledging Canada's higher standard of living. "One lives well, but a part of me I left behind in Italy. Even today I love Canada. I got my citizenship: I stand by Canada, but I love Italy. I would have liked to have become a nun, but today I'm happy the way I am, because had I been a nun I would have been closed up in a convent and I wouldn't do the good I'm doing today. Today instead I'm free, independent . . . the first days I was perturbed, but now I'm happy."

When I arrived, Genoveffa was at home with a friend, praying; they were doing *Via crucis*, the fourteen stations of the cross. Genoveffa was kneeling on the foot of her confessional, praying; her friend prayed along, sometimes replying, sometimes repeating verses. Within the small room there was an altar with various religious artifacts such as statues of St. Joseph, the Virgin Mary and others. Surrounding the numerous icons, rosary beads, flowers, candles and glass-cased statues there were plants and flowers. On the walls were photographs of family, along with pictures of Padre Pio (an Italian priest whose prayers are believed to have healed the sick). The room smelled of burning wax. As I was sitting, taking notes on this religious ceremony, Genoveffa's friend suspiciously asked me what I was writing. I assured her, and I think I managed to appease her concern. It was an unusual experience for me and I remember thinking how strange that this shrine lay in urban Montreal; it seemed incongruous. Genoveffa is a member of a religious sisterhood called *l'Armata di Maria* (the Sisters of Maria).

Before beginning the interview Genoveffa placed *pizzelle* (Italian waffle-shaped cookies) and *torrone* (Italian nougat candy) on the table. We drank coffee and chatted before starting. As we went along in the interview, Genoveffa would get up to show me photographs of the people and places she was talking about. She spoke freely of her life and didn't seem to have any reservations about being interviewed. Throughout the evening we were interrupted at several times by friends, neighbors and family.

Apart, Genoveffa's candor and animated personality, one of the most distinctive features of the interview was her ability to recall songs of all kinds. She had a repertoire of traditional Italian songs that included melodic love songs, lullabies and nursery rhymes. When singing, Genoveffa became flirtatious, moving her hands, batting her eyes and playing the part of the seductive young maiden. She sang most of the songs in her Neapolitan dialect.

The attitude expressed in Genoveffa's narrative suggests a pragmatic approach to both her social and emotional life. Although she openly discusses her overbearing husband and how he verbally abused her during his later years, she recalls this period with an accepting tone; she isn't bitter. Her personal interests keep her busy and involve her in the present. In her old age she sounds self-assured and happy; she is concerned with the business of living by pursuing her interest in serving *Dio* (God). After an incompatible marriage and years of caring for her dying husband, Genoveffa finds a great deal of personal satisfaction in religious activities. At eighty-five, she leads an active life, organizing and attending community affairs. Her faith has offered her a great deal of sustenance in the past, as well as the present. The renewed commitment to her religious convictions not only reaffirms her long-standing belief in the power of God, but also marks a new stage in Genoveffa's life – a period of great personal freedom and independence.

Graziella Di Corpo

Graziella Di Corpo was born in the town of Pollo in northern Italy. She is sixty-eight years old and has two sons and a daughter. For the last thirty-eight years she has lived in Montreal. Recently retired, she is an active member of Centro Donne, where we met for the interview.

Graziella's family moved to France after her father lost his job as a customs officer for breaking office policy and getting married; her mother worked as a nurse in a children's hospital. When Graziella was thirteen her mother died of tuberculosis. At that time her father decided to return to Italy and oversee the property that had belonged to his wife.

An only child, Graziella hardly ever saw her mother. For five years she lived at St. Vincent de Paul convent; she found life with the nuns regimented and cold. Although she experienced problems readjusting to the village when she returned to Italy to live with her grandmother, she felt there was a greater warmth and affection there.

At her grandmother's house, she remembers sitting around *il focolare* (the fireplace), listening to stories of Bertoldo, a trickster figure. As Graziella retold the perils of Bertoldo, ripples of laughter followed, usually ending with "Oh those were great stories." In both versions of the Bertoldo story, Bertoldo manages to outwit the king and save his life.

While Graziella's father went hunting she mostly stayed at home, sometimes going to visit women friends to sew and pass the time. Her father was very strict, allowing her only to go to church and participate in the choir. After his wife's death he never remarried.

When Graziella turned eighteen she was forced into a marriage that was not of her choosing. A great deal of anger and frustration is associated with this event. "They married me to a barber. They married me to a *barbiere*. They married me [*raises her voice*]. They married me. I was in Rome; it was an arranged marriage, after all eh [*sighs*] – ten months later I had a child."

As Graziella recalls, she was unprepared for married life. "I found myself lost, disoriented. First of all, in those days we didn't have any experience like the young women of today. I didn't know anything about men, nor of life. You find yourself like that suddenly. I found it bad. Then what are you going to do, I adapted."

During the war Graziella's village had been destroyed by bombs. Fed up with the war and what she calls miserable living conditions (*la miseria*), her family decided to leave for Canada. When they arrived, her aunt found an apartment for them with all the necessary amenities. Soon after, she had her third son.

Graziella has no regrets about coming to Canada. "I bless this country, I've been here thirty-eight years, problems I never had." With her husband's trade as a barber and her ability to speak French, her experiences in Montreal were favorable. At that time, however, Quebec was dominated by anglophones and she remembers her feelings of exclusion when people refused to speak French. "It was not a grand life, but we never went without the necessities."

After her children were grown, Graziella went into the labor market. Because she had no formal training, she found employment mostly in unskilled jobs. She remembers working in the plastics industry, cutting negatives at Direct Film, a photo developing company, and tagging garments at Reitman's, a women's clothing store.

Looking back, Graziella regrets having married so young. She feels that she never got to enjoy her *gioventù* (youth). While Graziella did not have the opportunity to pursue a singing career, today she enjoys singing in the church choir. Retired, she regularly attends the activities offered at Centro Donne.

Even though Graziella has visited Italy several times since her departure, she feels Canada is her home. "This is my adopted land, I've spent more years here. I found it to my liking."

While Graziella found village life "backward," she has fond memories of living with her grandmother, who played a surrogate mother role. Remembering the storytelling occasions around the *focolare*[8] brought back the special moments she and her grandmother shared. In retelling the wonderful serial stories of the trickster character, Bertoldo, one senses Graziella is reliving the experiences associated with this event.

In describing the context in which the stories took place, Graziella highlights the fireplace as the focal point around which people would congregate.

The story in this context is an event shared by people that holds personal and social meanings. Each time a story is retold, it is experienced anew and lives in the creative imaginations of the listener. As Graziella skillfully retells the stories of Bertoldo, she lets out hearty chuckles of laughter; she is completely involved, fascinated with the antics of this figure. In the stories of Bertoldo, the trickster outwits the authority figures, Graziella appears to have found strength and a means of coping with the limitations imposed upon her by her father and her society.

Gina Lorenzo

Born in Treviso, Italy, Gina is fifty-three years old and has lived in Canada for the last twenty years. Separated from her husband for several years, she receives welfare assistance to meet her living expenses. She has little contact with her daughter, an only child. When we met in her basement apartment, Gina was undergoing radiation treatment for throat cancer.[9]

In recalling her childhood years, Gina especially remembers the hardship and poverty her family experienced. One thing that stands out in her memory is the crowded housing. "I remember a great deal of poverty, too many people, too many cousins in a small home . . . and the sincere truth was that there wasn't much, and I am very proud today, because I know what it was like to be hungry."

Her parents did not allow her and her siblings to bring friends over because there were too many people sharing the household. "They were very strict, they didn't let us out, they didn't let us out – closed, very regimented; we weren't allowed to bring friends, there were too many people." Even though they did not have a great deal to eat, she said, they were happy. "With some potatoes and corn meal (*polenta*) we ate nonetheless," she said.

For leisure Gina remembers how the men played cards in the barn by themselves, while the women chatted among themselves. One of her favorite games was hopscotch (*campana*). "Before, the smallest thing was a toy, today a small pebble isn't much."

Prompted by the mention of pebbles, Gina recalls the time she threw a stone at her father's bird cage, causing the cage to fall and the birds to die. "I remember my father punishing me. There were some birds in a cage. He used to go hunt these birds and put them in the cage and, ping pong, I hits the cage down on the floor and the birds die. He spanked me so hard that I pissed in my pants." Another meaningful incident, one which Gina is ashamed of telling me about at first, is the time she had cut up her mother's Sunday shoes. To this day she finds it hard to forgive herself for the spiteful way she behaved. "I can't tell you about the awful thing I did to mother, she was very hurt. For the rest of my life I will remember it almost as if it were today. The shoes were very sacred because we were poor. She punished me, I was seven years old, stubborn."

At thirteen Gina was sent to Milan to work as a live-in maid. Scared and lonely, she longed to be with her family. "Thirteen years old, you leave your mother, your parents. I felt very sad to see them only a year later. The tears I shed were mine. At night for bedtime I was by myself."

She sent money back home to her parents and used to leave some money aside for what she called small indulgences (*capricci*). By the time Gina was twenty years old she had worked in several places – Rome, Milan and even in Switzerland. Both she and her older sister were in Switzerland at the same time, employed as domestic workers. They shared a strong bond and her sister played the role of surrogate mother. "My sister always taught me, the straight path (*la strada diritta*). We were in Switzerland together. We would go out, she would accompany me. She too was a domestic worker and on Saturday she would come to pick me up. I was protected even though I was without my mother." For the most part, Gina found her work oppressive and unsatisfying. She felt she was always being watched; without any time for herself, she was constantly answering to someone.

When she was twenty years old she was married by proxy, her father signing on her behalf. With a harsh tone of voice and a blank look in her face, Gina's statement at the outset of the interview bitterly describes how her marriage occurred: "Twenty years emigrated, married by proxy, signature from Dad."

Two months after her arrival in Montreal, Gina was pregnant. Because she had been ill, she lost the child. Since then she has had various medical problems. Her second child was born shortly after and

Gina describes this as the beginning of her "apartment life."

During her years as a housewife, she sometimes babysat other people's children. Some years after she and her husband separated, she boarded with an older man whom she took care of until he died.

When Gina and I met she was midway through the radiation treatment for her throat cancer. Suffering from hair loss, she wore a wig. As she sat next to the kitchen table, and I on the small couch in the kitchen, we talked about the study I was doing.

At the beginning of the interview, Gina was quite reticent, even hostile. When I asked her to repeat or explain something she would raise her voice at me. She often lost patience correcting my choice of words. There appeared to be the attitude that, as a Northerner, her Italian was correct. Often she resorted to her dialect and accent making it difficult for me to understand her. After about one hour of taping we stopped for a break. At that point the tone became more relaxed. Gina started to open up. In fact, some time after the first session, she took me in her confidence by describing the incident with the shoes.

As the interview progressed, Gina's tone became softer. During the break she made me coffee and gave me some cookies. In the span of two hours there had been a transformation. I went from being treated as a strange intruder to being treated as a friendly visitor. Only a short while before I had felt like I was being attacked, and now the same woman showed me kindness. I was amazed at the fluidity of the situation.

Asking Gina to speak about her life was not easy. It involved discussing intimate matters which she probably would have preferred left unspoken. Although she seemed to censor her conversation in some areas, she shared many painful memories.

There appears to have been a lack of warmth in Gina's upbringing. Because of crowded living conditions, Gina could not bring friends home and had little opportunity to develop relationships. The incident with the shoes and the story of her father's spanking suggest an emotionally stark childhood. These narratives also suggest a young child's call for attention in a situation where the main concern was with survival and not necessarily with well-being. Her proxy marriage, with her father signing on her behalf, further accentuates the fact that individual rights were not a primary consideration under those circumstances. Resentment and bitterness were voiced in regard to this decision and, when recalling the incident, Gina conveyed the information in a cold manner.

The supportive mother-surrogate presence in Gina's life was her older sister. She shared a close bond with her, appreciating her guidance, protection and teaching of the straight path (*la strada diritta*). The pursuit of chastity and the protection of one's virginity against sexual overtures are especially significant here, as domestic workers were frequently considered sexually promiscuous.

Implicit throughout Gina's narrative is the fear

of male intrusion and the outside world. Gina's preoccupation with the safety of her daughter illustrates this point. Like her mother before her, Gina tried to provide her daughter with the strict upbringing she had received. She remembers losing sleep worrying about her daughter's safety. She comments on the clash between the traditional mores of village life and the freer North American standards: "The young people in Montreal are not like us; we were from the village, followed examples by being careful and making sure we were always accompanied, and told to be careful (*di fare attenzione*)." She warns me of the pain a mother feels when her daughter resists her will. She points her finger at me: "If you as a daughter mistreat your mother, poor you, Giovanna, poor you, Giovanna."

Gina expresses little trust and confidence in people. "After much time has gone by I wish to be alone. I like company but little – everyone in their homes (*ognuno per conto suo*). Domestic work is always done alone. It's unfortunate, but like this you remain isolated. So it's better to be alone than to keep in bad company. Why should I trust a friend who will betray me? I look at myself in the mirror and I say: 'Gina, take care of your own personal business, don't be jealous.' "

Finding comfort in her solitude and believing in the supreme power of God, she feels that He alone decides our destiny. "He creates you and He takes you back."

Brought face to face with her mortality by throat cancer, Gina does not hold high expectations for the future. "Now my life is that of an old poor woman. Today I understand more, one shouldn't think of abundance, everything comes and goes." Though the medical prognosis for the throat cancer is good, she has lost a great deal of weight from the radiation treatment. Because of her illness Gina declined to have her photograph taken.

Bitterness and resentment are expressed throughout Gina's narrative. Separated from her husband and estranged from her daughter, she faces her illness with only the support of a few friends. Her resigned attitude, faith in God and her own resources are her sole sources of comfort.

Francesca Mancini

"All men are swine."

Francesca Mancini was born in 1911. Her family lived in Lama dei Peligni, a town in the Abruzzo region of Italy. One of five siblings, she is seventy-eight years old, has three married children and lives in what is commonly known in Montreal as the Greek Area. Strongly religious, she attends Church regularly.

Francesca's mother was a seamstress and sewed clothes at home. Her husband was a sojourner miner in Pennsylvania. When he returned to volunteer for the war, he was refused because of asthma. At first this was a time of hardships. "We got back on our feet." Her husband became a fruit vendor. "He would go sell fruit in the town of Perry Como," she jokes. Later, when her father died, the family moved to the countryside to look after the land. Francesca's parents both died at a young age, her father at thirty-four and her mother at thirty-nine.

In 1934, after being engaged for nine years, she married Camillo Mancini. Like her mother, Francesca was trained in the art of sewing (*arte di cucire*), but she was forced to stop because her father died. She had to take care of her twin sisters and cook the family meals because her mother was in the countryside working. "Every night I had to cook potatoes at my mother's house. We were poor."

After a two-week trip on the ship *Atlantica*, Francesca joined her husband in January of 1953, two years after his arrival. Once in Montreal she started to work almost immediately. Like many Italian immigrants she sent money back home to her family. "Imagine, I made thirteen dollars the first day." For a year she worked in a women's accessories factory where she made jewelry. Her second and last job was with the factory Jocardi where she was promoted to "forelady." Francesca has fond memories of her workdays at the factory. It provided a place where Italian immigrant women could exchange thoughts and concerns. As they stitched their garments the women improvised wordplay, shared stories about families and immigration and participated in the delightfully irreverent activity of mock swearing. "Sometimes we used to fight," Francesca adds.

Francesca still feels strong ties with her native country, albeit, after thirty-five years, she feels that Canada is her home. Though she remembers with shame not knowing how to speak French when she first arrived, she now manages with the language and can make herself understood. As for her first impressions of Quebec: "There wasn't a bit of snow, but a biting cold."

On the day I went to interview Francesca, my aunt and uncle accompanied me; aunt Rosilda and Francesca had worked together in the same factory. When we arrived at her home she greeted us at the door and showed us into the kitchen. As is the custom with visitors, she offered us espresso coffee and sweets. Following a brief explanation of my study, she proudly commented on how she had been interviewed by a reporter on her immigrant experiences and was not new to being interviewed.

Before beginning the interview, she provided her guests with a tour of her home. While showing us the different rooms she often pointed out particular photographs and special objects, sometimes relating an anecdote associated with a memento. Every object had its own story, spurring various memories and observations. For example, the big television set in the corner of the small living room prompted the story of the time they were burglarized. After this tour, a symbolic expression of welcome, we went back to the kitchen to begin the interview.

Her home reminded me of the many houses I had visited when I was growing up. The knitted doilies on the couch and multicolored knitted covers over the pillows, the doll that lay on the center of the bed and ceramic tiles that covered most of the kitchen walls were typical of the inner furnishings of many Italian immigrant dwellings in Montreal. For me they were cultural markers reminding me of specific events in my own life, such as the time my mother sewed an ornate dress for the doll that was to be placed on my bed.

In some Italian immigrant homes, the hosts, as a gesture of hospitality, literally and figuratively open up their houses to visitors. This is a way of formally expressing who they are. By sharing their intimate space they extend a sign of friendship. As some researchers have pointed out, this is the public face of the household and, as such, makes a public statement.[10] A clean house, for instance, reflects well upon the housekeeping abilities of the wife – especially in traditional Italian society where the home is a major source of identification for the woman. Because I was specifically interested in women's expressive behavior, I requested that my uncle leave the room. After some coaxing by his wife, who told him, "This is women stuff, it doesn't concern you," he went into the living room grumbling and wondering what we could possibly talk about that would require his absence.

Having survived this minor hurdle, I sat at the kitchen table with Francesca and my aunt, who was quiet and only occasionally interjected comments. Throughout the interview Francesca was keenly aware of her audience, manipulating her voice, pointing her finger to stress a point and contorting her face. She enjoyed telling stories, riddles and jokes; she especially took pleasure in participating in obscene verbal bantering, playfully telling dirty jokes and riddles. Stories like "The Jokester" – which describes the time she tricked her husband into giving her the chair closest to the heater – and "The Time the Germans Came" – which describes of how she and her family escaped death during World War II – demonstrate her mischievous spirit and readiness to turn the mundane and ordinary into a festive occasion (see *Appendix*, Mancini).

Francesca quickly established her proclivity toward comic irreverence and boisterous behavior by proclaiming at the beginning of our taped conversation that "all men are swine." This was emblematic of her style and demeanor. On another level, however, this opening line clearly operated as one part of a private performance. In this "narrative event," Francesca used the rabble-rouser image as a stylistic device to shock, entertain, and, above all, affirm our shared sisterhood. I knew from Francesca's delivery that I was not to take this outrageous statement at face value. The implicit message said, "We understand one another, we are both women." Moreover, as a comment on my uncle's begrudging acceptance of her request to leave the room, the line "all men are swine" at once excluded him from the sisterhood and tied her narrative to the immediate context of the interview.

That day, on the ride back to my place, my uncle gently scolded me for not interviewing men. I tried to justify my research by telling him that there were plenty of studies that dealt with the experiences of men, and that I wanted a women's take on the world. At that moment I remembered the silent reproach my father expressed during the time I spent working on my research.[11]

Francesca had fond memories of her workdays at the factory. They seemed to provide a place where Italian immigrant women could exchange thoughts and concerns. There, the women improvised wordplays, shared stories and participated in the delightfully irreverent activity "mock swearing."

Such types of verbal art are quite similar to the ritual insults, verbal sparring and "rhetoric of exaggeration" that folklore scholars have observed among Afro-Americans;[12] stemming from an occupational setting, both the Italian-Canadian and Afro-American interactions work as a cohesive force in affirming group identity. Most importantly, while the factory work in which Francesca was engaged was by no means easy, it served a variety of important functions in her life, giving her her own source of income and connecting her to a vital community of women.

CHAPTER THREE

To Walk the Straight Path

Gender and Subversion in Italian Women's Folklore

Toward the end of my study, it became clear that relationships between men and women in Italian life were governed by the idea that women are a force that must be controlled and contained. Many of the songs from the Old Country metaphorically spoke of the potential dangers of women when left to their own devices. My conversations with these women displayed both a reverence for and disquieting fear of the female gender in Italian culture.

In this chapter I will explore how this assumption has played itself out in certain key themes in the women's narratives. First, I will explore the theme of forced seclusion; discussed in all the interviews, the highly restrictive practice of forced seclusion stems directly from the assumption that women need constant supervision. In the next section, I will examine how women respond to such social and cultural constraints through songs, lullabies, riddles and stories of tricksters and witches. While the theme of forced seclusion speaks to the suppression of women, the second section examines the creative ways women challenge and resist traditional Italian society.

Forced Seclusion

> "Back in those days it wasn't the custom to go out."
> Stefania Annibale

"Life was too closed in, we couldn't go out, no, no, no, for nothing, home and church." This statement illustrates a common life experience among the women I interviewed and reflects the sexually restrictive climate often found in Mediterranean culture. This section analyses the views, beliefs and values connected with the practice of "forced seclusion." More importantly, here I try to understand how Italian immigrant women experience this form of repression.

There is a great deal of evidence suggesting that women's choices in traditional Italian society are largely influenced by men.[1] Studies dealing with Italian traditional cultural patterns show that until married, women live in a predominantly female environment where interaction with the opposite sex often is supervised and takes place under formal circumstances.[2] Historian Franca Iacovetta argues that "because of the high premium placed on women's chastity and family honor, community surveillance is a central feature of life in the towns, consequently from puberty a woman is confined to the home" and insulated from the forces of the outside world.[3]

"Even when she marries," writes scholar Inez Free-man-Cardozo, "she is discouraged from leaving the house unaccompanied and from having other women companions; only women in the immediate family are allowed into her circle. This restriction is maintained to protect the honor of the husband."[4]

In commenting on the repressive society of her time, Antonietta voiced resentment and tempered hostility when she recalls her life in Giovinazzo. "I was watched," she said, "even sometimes my brother would try to convince my mother to let me go with him. He was young and would tell my mother: 'If I don't bring an escort, they won't let me in the dance.' My mother would say: 'If you go, go, but my daughter is staying here.' "

Here, Antonietta clearly expresses her dislike of containment, but in the same interview she expresses satisfaction that, unlike other young women, her own daughter doesn't go out. By staying home, her daughter provides her with companionship and assures her that she is safe from harm and remains a good girl (*una buona ragazza*).

With Gina Lorenzo, in particular, the experience of forced seclusion and isolation is compounded by her occupation as a live-in domestic worker. Having left her family at the young age of thirteen, she felt especially vulnerable and feared the potential harm that men represent. Alone in a big city, away from the security of her family and working in a job that was full of stigma, this young single woman experienced a particularly heightened fear of male intrusion.

Such fears are also accentuated by the traditional rules of Italian life that Gina brought with her to the city. The often repeated warning is to walk the straight path (*fare la strada diritta*). This catch-all phrase, meaning literally to follow the straight path, invokes a variety of rules, the foremost of which is the proscription against any sexual contact or taint. Throughout the interviews, Gina expresses difficulties with such cultural pressures. When she got to the city, instead of being under the close scrutiny of her father or brother, she was now having to answer to another paternalistic authority figure – her boss (*il padrone*). "The boss watches over you on all levels, they're like cops; they spy on you and watch you and they comment on the time you come back home. What did you do? Did you have fun? If you don't tell them the truth you risk losing your job, you have to be honest in everything."

This passage echoes the suspicion concerning the moral character of women in her profession. One of the folk beliefs associated with domestic workers is that they are promiscuous (*facili*). Therefore, to be treated with suspicion and contempt is the employers' prerogative, if not their obligation. "Domestic work is always done alone. It's unfortunate, but like this you remain isolated, disillusioned, so it's better, better to be alone, than to keep with bad company."

While a double standard made it acceptable for men to engage in premarital and extramarital sexual relations, the "fallen" woman brought shame to herself and to the whole family. "Women are [seen as] the weaker or baser sex and if left unguarded, they easily give way to looser morals and promiscuity,"[5] writes Iacovetta in describing visions of womanhood. "Consequently, few women enjoyed, for instance, socializing in the piazza unless accompanied by male escorts."[6] Women's activities are usually organized around the home, sometimes involving specific female rituals such as sewing sessions, embroidery or cooking. A woman's culture is evident in the "numerous bonds women formed with other female relatives and close neighbors."[7] Criticizing the belief that women should stay in the private sphere Anna Del Negro said: "Men went out more often. They could go out. I wanted to go to San Buono [a neighboring town], but he [father] wouldn't let me."

In a more extreme case, Genoveffa Della Zazzera's husband prevented his daughter from attending high school. "The school was too far, then my husband being Italian, going out in the evening, mmh [*smiles*], you know Italians, always very strict." Going out in the evening was seen as inappropriate behavior for a young woman.

Reiterating a similar experience, Graziella Di Corpo commented on the jealousy that motivated the forced seclusion of women. In a bitter, sarcastic tone she said: "You know how fathers were back in those days. They were jealous, they wouldn't let us out. I would go only to the Catholic Mission and the choir."

Since male pride and honor is so closely tied up with the man's capacity to act "as an official representative with the wider community,"[8] keeping a close reign on wives and daughters is a means of preserving family honor and respectability; failure to do so is a disgrace. Losing face meant public humiliation and cast a doubt on the integrity of the entire family.

Guiding the cultural practice of forced seclusion in traditional Italian society is the belief that women are to be feared and supervised. With their ability to reproduce, women control the blood line of the community, an important commodity in a society of scarce resources. By keeping women hidden and isolated, their reproductive power is appropriated, controlled and contained. Inside, the woman is protected and in her "natural element;" outside, she is in a hostile environment. In the context of these ideas, a symbolic universe begins to unfold. Woman equals inside, a passive receptacle waiting to be fertilized, while the man is associated with the outside world, representing the active principle. Worshiped for her life-giving qualities, she is an earth-bound Madonna who remains immaculate and pristine, even when married. The other side of this Madonna image is the "whore" (*sfacciata*, which literally means "one without face"), a shameless woman who breaks the taboos that define the "proper woman."

This duality is also found in references made to day and night. Against strict orders from her grandmother, Stefania Annibale remembers going off with friends while it was still daylight outside; however, being out at night was unthinkable even for the most rebellious. The following personal experience narrative suggests that in the evening, another code of ethics operates. Describing the night as forbidden territory, Stefania Annibale said: "We used to go out in two or three's during the day, but if ever you went out at night – oh my! [*raising her voice*] – never in the night . . . 'Beware, don't go out, somebody will harm you' [her grandmother used to say]. She didn't want me to go out, when she wasn't around I would go, but I wouldn't go out in the evening." Conjuring up a world of dark and invisible forces, the night is symbolically associated with the fear of being violated and the loss of both personal and social control.

On the whole, the experiences of women are deeply influenced by the cautionary tales[9] and lore that warns them of the dangers that await them lest they comply with social expectations. Sometimes the source of evil is clearly identified. Anna who said, "You have to be careful of boys, if you go with young men you can no longer marry." At other times, the forces that threaten women were not clearly defined. In either case, these women were always told that the entire foundation of the community would be demolished if they dared defy the society's norms. In a rural setting where survival depends on allegiance to the group, going against the unwritten sexual taboos would be like desecrating family, church and motherhood. In a society of limited resources where everyone is assigned a specific role and task, the dissenter is not tolerated, especially if the dissenter is relegated to a subordinate position in the social hierarchy. The underlying message is that women had a precarious place in the world and little control over their lives.

Where gender segregation is part of a belief system that values female virginity, the forced seclusion of women becomes a social necessity. Highlighting the fear of sexual pollution that might come from mixing with boys, Anna remembers being prohibited from playing the popular stick and ball game (*curso*): "Back then they thought it was a scandal for girls and boys to be together, the old people thought of bad things. They were picky, the smallest things they gossiped."

Even though the women I interviewed are critical of this type of social control, the idea that women must protect themselves from "spoilage" still prevails. In much of the women's criticisms, what seems on the surface to be a call for the subversion of traditional beliefs is actually the reaffirmation of patriarchal ideas – particularly the idea of female chastity as something to be cherished and guarded. What women are challenging in these narratives is not the belief in abstinence before marriage, but the severe restrictions on the choices and activities of women in a male-dominated culture. In their criticism of the practice of forced seclusion, women are calling into question men's control over their bodies and not the traditional belief in sexual purity.

Even within this limiting patriarchal society where women's behavior and actions are closely scrutinized and restricted, women find different

ways of criticizing and subverting the established
order. In the following section, we will see how
women use folklore to transmit covert messages
concerning their society. The folktales, songs and
riddles found below represent an ongoing symbolic
discourse on gender and Italian traditional culture
as viewed from the New World.

Resistance through Folklore in Everyday Life: Songs of Forbidden Love

Directly or indirectly, a great deal of the lore in this
book centers on female sexuality. More than any
other, the folk song is the most popular means of
conveying messages about the consequences of forbidden love and the role of women in traditional
Italian society. In such a society, if women aren't
being simultaneously celebrated and ostracized for
defying taboo laws, they are presented as innocent
child/temptresses with witch-like magical powers
that disarm and entice the opposite sex.

One lyrical song specifically talks about a male
who has fallen under the spell of a young woman
called Marusella. In a soft, lamenting, hypnotic tone
Anna sings:

Marusella, Marusella,
se mesa l'aqua nel lu vino.
Ho perse o cuor,
Mia Abruzzese, oh mia Abruzzese.
Se tant dolce . . .

(Marusella, Marusella,
You put water in my wine.
I lost my heart,
Oh my Abruzzese, oh my Abruzzese
You are so sweet . . .)

On one level, a warning of the control young maidens have over men, this song also alludes to the forbidden pleasures of all-consuming passion. Despite the implied resistance, the young man is falling uncontrollably into a state of sin. The lyrics are sung from that man's perspective, and Anna conveys his bedazzlement by singing in a low-pitched, almost drunken tone. As the voice becomes softer, one senses that the singer is intoxicated, being lulled into a deep sleep, defenseless against the powers of the young girl.

Further, the amount of ecstasy derived from this fall seems directly linked to the extent to which it deviates from socially acceptable norms. In this song one can vicariously experience the pleasures of sexual taboo-breaking while not having to bear the punishment. Even though this song highlights the passionate love of an anticipated sexual encounter, the listener is reminded that there has been "foul play," that essentially this type of behavior is not condoned within the ordinary frames of Italian culture.

The image of the water in the wine supports this view. As folklorist Alessandro Falassi points out, wine holds a special iconographic meaning in Italian folk culture; it has been linked with a source of sustenance and nutrition: "Truth is believed to be located in wine."[10] By the same token, Falassi argues that water is often conceived by Italians as anti-matter,[11] an opposite to life. In terms of this symbolism, by adding water to the wine the young girl in the story disrupts the order of things, the former neutralizing and polluting the latter's life-giving potential.

Embodied in this song are both a celebration of sexual transcendence and an affirmation of abstinence. Such songs are means of flirting with the unpredictable, chaotic force of lust without threatening the status quo. Mediating tensions, the song serves a dual function: it provides an escape valve from the psychological pressures of society, and it articulates the social order by defining which activities are proscribed. From a didactic point of view, the song teaches about the rules of sexual behavior, as well as the pleasures derived from breaking those rules. These songs express the polarities of culture by trying to reconcile the contradictory forces of wild, lustful passions with the more tamed, socially approved expressions of the sexual impulse. In these songs women are depicted in a negative light. The song gives credence to the belief that women must be isolated because they unleash the libidinal impulses of men, impulses which pose a fundamental threat to patriarchal social structure.

Other songs, like "Sopra la poltrona" (On the Couch) sung by Anna Del Negro provide further evidence for the belief that women are to be feared, supervised and controlled. Criticizing the alleged actions of a young woman, the lyrics of this song read:

E sopra la poltrona
se saggiat qualcosa buono
che mo de na po scorda.
Nannin sei tanto bella, Nannin sei tanto buona.
A bal pa' San Giovanni ci se incontrata
e la gente c' ha criticata che tu eri na sfacciata.

(And on the couch
You tasted something good.
It was so good that you can't forget.
Nannin, you' re so beautiful, Nannin, you are so good.
Down by San Giovanni we met
and people's gossip said you were a shame less hussy.)

This song is reminiscent of those sung in public defamation rituals (*charivari*) commonly found in seventeenth-century Europe. In the spirit of amusement and protest against those who broke codes of conduct, villagers express their disapproval by burning effigies, placing foul-smelling shrubs in front of the person's house and singing slanderous songs or mocking riddles.[12] Like the *charivari*, contemporary narrative songs (*stornelli*) such as "Sopra la poltrona" are intended to damage one's respectability.[13] Often such slanderous accusations reflect competition between two or more men in acquiring the graces of a woman. My mother's interpretation of the song agrees with Falassi's argument. She especially highlights the malicious intentions behind such songs. These folk songs also provide the background to occupational situations. One can speculate that, while the mocking *stornelli* reported by my mother are originally a means of voicing disapproval, it might well be sung on other occasions, such as on the daily trek to the well to get fresh water.

A refrain from another song refers to the burden that comes with "carnal knowledge." The imagery is that of the forbidden fruit of the Garden of Eden. Through sexual contact a certain kind of symmetry and perfection is broken, broken by an act for which the woman appears to take the entire blame. The suggestion is that once a woman has experienced sexuality, she is transformed and is unable to return to her original state of innocence. Genoveffa sings:

> Ca s'occio di veluta,
> ho pers o cuor.
> E mammata ne sappeva
> e da na pu scorda.

> (With those velvet eyes
> I lost my heart.
> And your mother didn't know about it,
> And now you can't forget.)
> I want to kiss you but . . .)

In an other song, Genoveffa sings:

> Scti dormende bel e fresche,
> dorme e sofia dentro lu giardin' . . .
> Ca la carne bel e fresche,
> ch se treche nera.
> Se mis dentro cuor mille pensier malamente.

> (You're sleeping nice and fresh,
> Sleepin' and sighin'.
> You go in this here garden . . .

. . . This nice fresh flesh,
And those black braids.
You put in my heart one thousand evil thoughts.)

Beyond the biblical references to the Garden of
Eden, we again see a pubescent girl depicted as dangerous; she unconsciously sows evil in her midst by
provoking lustful yearnings in men. The tension
between the physical urges (unknowingly spurred
by the mere presence of the girl) and the "immoral"
thoughts crossing the man's mind adds to the feelings of urgency conveyed by this song. This song
appears to be a covert way of talking about the
power of sexual attraction, at least from a male
viewpoint. It also suggests that the female is especially desirable during puberty. At this "neither/nor"
stage, she is no longer a girl but not yet a woman.

For the most part, the songs are tied to
courtship rituals and, as Falassi observed in the folk
songs from the Tuscany region, they express the
various stages in the development of love without
being too explicit or causing embarrassment. In
many ways, the songs support the idea that women
are to be closely watched and segregated from men;
otherwise they will cause havoc. It is assumed that
men and women can not be left alone in the same
room without some sexual transgression.

Although muted, a misogynist tendency reveals
itself in these folk songs. In this sexually repressive
society the female is not readily approachable or
knowable. She is mysterious and unpredictable, like
the mythical Hindu goddess Kali. Like the forces of

nature, her energy needs to be harnessed and dominated, in this case, by a patriarchal ideology that
ensures control over her body, behavior and per-
sonhood.

Yet these songs are sung by and for women. The
themes of seduction and sexual transgression ultimately belie a complex cultural process that involve
both subversive and oppressive messages. The songs
of forbidden love celebrate the power of female
sexuality by repeatedly depicting male characters as
overwhelmed by a woman's charms.[14] However,
the vision of female sexuality so celebrated reiter-
ates the assumption that women are an anarchic
force that requires containment. Ironically, the
assumption which these women reiterate is the very
idea that informs and legitimates the most oppressive practices of traditional Italian society – forced
seclusion and constant supervision. Women's folklore both rails against patriarchy and helps to perpetuate its most cherished ideas.

More paradoxical is the literary articulation of
these ideas. In all of these Songs of Forbidden Love,
the song is sung from the perspective of the overwhelmed man. Thus, in the symbolic universe of the
song, the women are able to tout the power of their
sexuality in the most intense manner – by making
their fantasized victims (the men) sing of the power
of the female. In the Songs of Forbidden Love, the
women are able to achieve the ultimate reversal: not
only are women dominant, they also make men
importantly bemoan their powerlessness.

What could speak more clearly of these

women's desire for personal autonomy, if not revenge and social privilege? It is most ironic that the device by which women achieve ultimate power in the symbolic world – the unbridled might of female sexuality – is precisely the idea which is used to constrain them in the real world. The coexistence of rebellion and submission in women's folklore reflects the deeper contradictions of Italian gender politics.

Lullabies as Critique of Motherhood

A haunting and disturbing subtext reveals itself in some of the lullabies collected in this study. While some lullabies are cheerful and appear to celebrate the mother/child relationship as a joyous event, other songs convey feelings of sorrow. The lullaby "Rag Doll" speaks of a mother who has left her child with the grandmother. The song expresses the grandmother's misplaced resentment toward the child for having to be cared for, while the mother is gone to a village celebration (*festa*). Genoveffa sings:

> Ninnao.
> A nonna la puppa di pezze,
> peche mamma eh iuta a la festa.
> Quant torna mamma, la puppeta tornera.
> Ninnao.

> (To your grandmother [goes] the rag doll,
> Because your mother has gone to the *festa*.
> When mommy returns, the little dolly she will return.)

The song describes how, in the absence of the mother, a rag doll has been taken away from the child. This suggests an element of punishment. Later, however, the void left by the mother's departure is made complete by her return, when she brings with her the rag doll that had been taken away.

While indirectly speaking of the confusion and helplessness the child might feel in the mother's absence and covertly voicing the mother's anxieties about separation, this lullaby also makes a statement about the place of the mother in Italian traditional culture. Going to the *festa* implies a disruption in the natural order of things. It is only after a restitution occurs that normality is reestablished. The imagery here is of abandonment and anticipated reunion.

Although it is difficult to articulate with clarity the disturbing mood evoked by some of the lullabies, one immediately senses the private reflection on the meaning of motherhood. In the soothing, sorrowful sounding lullaby "Dormi, dormi" this is most evident. A feeling of loss, even despair, is conveyed. In a sense the mother appears to be grieving for the child who enters the world of sleep. She remembers the child by telling her that "your mommy is next to you." The song expresses the closeness shared between mother and child, while alluding to what one scholar has called the "mother's conversation with herself about separation."[15]

One lullaby explicitly refers to giving the child away. Invoking the frightening imagery, the text speaks of giving the child to the old hag (*befana*) for

the week and then "the bogeyman" for the month.
Francesca remembers singing this lullaby to her
daughter Lucia.

> Ninnao, ninnao,
> bella bambina che ho.
> E se la befana viene ti darò a lei,
> per la settimana, e se l'uomo torna,
> lui t'avrà per tutto il mese.
> Ninnao, ninnao.

> (Ninnao, ninnao,
> Nice child that I have.
> If the old witch comes,
> I will give you to her,
> For the week, and if the bogeyman comes,
> He'll have you for a whole month.
> Ninnao, ninnao.[16]

By shifting attention away from the content, the listener hears the happy melodic tune of the lullaby
without attending to the meaning of the text.[17] Lullabies sometimes disguise a distressing message with
pretty melodies and rhythms.[18]

While this lullaby may be intended for the
enjoyment of the child, on a deeper level the singer
entertains the notion of giving the child away – an
idea that would be totally unacceptable if voiced in
public. Through this song, the caretaker can relieve
her frustration without directly challenging traditional notions of motherhood in Italian culture.

By both revealing and hiding these personal and
social messages, the lullaby is a gender-specific
genre through which women, consciously or uncon-

sciously, express their ambivalence toward motherhood. As many scholars have noted, lullabies can be
a way of speaking about the unspeakable without
being ostracized from the community.

Flirting with Danger: The Obscene Riddle

> "All men are swine!"
> Francesca Mancini

Playing on taboos and fears of sexual pollution,
Francesca Mancini told me a riddle which teases the
mind with misleading sexual innuendo. With the
skill of a trickster character from *la commedia
dell'arte*, Francesca asks:

> All women have one underneath. Some have it whole,
> some have it broken [*misleading sexual overtone*]. Some
> have it dirty and some have it clean. And not more than
> four fingers. Answer: The hem of a suit. More than four
> fingers you can't have a hem [*showing me with her fin-
> gers and raising her eyebrows*].

The deceptive imagery refers to the female genitals,
yet the listener is tricked into thinking that the
answer has something to do with the hymen, a sup-
posed physical marker for female chastity. Therefore, when the teller alludes to "some women have
it whole, some women have it broken," one is lead
to believe that virginity and the loss of virginity is
part of the equation. Further clues of "some have it
dirty, some have it clean" support this conclusion
(that is, dirty equals sexual contact, clean equals

sexual purity). What makes this solution even more plausible is the phallic symbolism reflected in the statement "not more than four fingers."

Fraught with sexual overtones, the entertaining quality of this riddle lies in its ability to poke fun at social conventions by bringing the taboo-laden subject of chastity and virginity into the public sphere. All along one thinks: "Oh no, she can't possibly be referring to that." When faced with the answer (hem) we are made to feel foolish by the harmless simplicity of the solution. Part of the fun comes in showing us how logical thinking leads us into drawing analogies between two unrelated things: chastity and hem.

Furthermore, the riddle is an imaginative way of talking about the unspeakable and turning a highly serious and tabooed matter upside down. By symbolically inverting patriarchal views of female sexuality, women engage in an act of reclaiming control and autonomy over their bodies. They enter a space in which they take chances with new roles and ideas. The cultural boundaries that frame everyday life are suspended, turned topsy turvy and playfully rearranged. This playful riddle is a

> means of inducing play, that is the freeing up of fused energies within a restrictive or artificial environment in which social threat can paradoxically be expressed without threatening.[20]

Riddles are believed to perform many functions, psychological and social. They have been attributed with strengthening the ego of the riddler, sometimes at the expense of the listener.[21] Francesca was keenly aware of her privileged position, laughing at the confused look on my face as I tried to come up with the answer. Not only are riddles entertaining pastimes, but as Falassi and others have pointed out, they are instructive. They teach the young about society, metaphorical speech and verbal skills.

Some recent writers have found a series of interesting obscene riddles that had embarrassed earlier collectors in the past. Many of these riddles had "hidden sexual meanings or seemed to indicate an obscene answer, sexual or otherwise, while the correct answer was . . . innocent."[22] One folklorist classifies this type as "pretend obscene riddles," because they tantalize the listener with sexual innuendo, yet deliver a tame answer.[23]

> Playing riddles allowed one to speak, and not to speak, to pronounce dirty and obscene words, to propose tendential and malicious definition, sometimes emphasized by a look, a wink, a sign, or half smile.[24]

Given the highly intimate setting of the interview and the taboo subject of the riddle, I felt that by sharing her riddles with me Francesca was allowing me to enter a sort of private female world. Outside of this context, I suspect this riddle would be censored, or, depending on the situation, it would have held different levels of meanings.

From the outset, Francesca established her joking manner by starting the taped interview with the pronouncement "All men are swine." Once again, I believe she was giving me her seal of approval and affirming our shared sisterhood. Later, playing to an audience, she amusingly referred to her vast repertoire of obscene words in order to stress a point or simply to entertain the guest. Like other women I spoke with, she derived an almost cathartic pleasure in flirting with the socially unacceptable by participating in obscene verbal bantering.

Breaking All the Rules: Bertoldo

> "Oh, those were great stories."
> Graziella Di Corpo

At her grandmother's house during the winter, Graziella Di Corpo remembered sitting around the fireplace (*il focolare*) listening to stories of the king's abbot, Bertoldo. As Graziella retold the perils of Bertoldo, ripples of laughter followed, usually ending with "Oh, those were great stories."

Bertoldo the Trickster

There was a fool (*buffone*). There was this king that could not get rid of him in any way. One evening my grandmother told me that they had put him on the roof of the house to make him die from the cold. Instead what did he do. All evening he worked moving things around – flower pots. He moved one thing and then another. This made him perspire and fight off the cold. In the morning the kings men found Bertoldo alive. One time they fixed a big supper for the king. The king was in the kitchen the day his special meal was being prepared. They had prepared chicken. All the chickens had a leg missing. Therefore, when it came time to serve chicken to the king's guests, the guests looked at the chicken and noticed that the legs were missing. The king was furious. He went to the kitchen and demanded to know who had done this. The cook said, "*Signor eccellenza*, Your excellence, I know who did it. It was Bertoldo, he ate them all." The king exclaimed, "How could he disgrace me so in front of my guests." Bertoldo said, "But they only had one leg?" "How could you," said the king. "Come, come" – and they went into the courtyard. The chickens were cold because it was winter and they have the habit of tucking one leg under their wing. "So every chicken has one leg missing, see," Bertoldo said. The king claps his hands, startling the chicken into putting their other leg down. The king said, "How do you figure they only have one leg?" "Oh they have two, Master," Bertoldo says dumbfounded. He did a thousand and one tricks. That poor king [*laughter*]. So the king said, "You will have to hang for this, I'll make you pay for this. I want you dead." Bertoldo said, "You must grant me one last wish; let me choose the tree from which I will hang." The king said, "Okay, you have been granted your wish." So Bertoldo said, "I want to be hung from a parsley tree." They had to send him back.

In both stories Bertoldo managed to outwit the king and save his life. Although the king was exasperated with Bertoldo's antics he could not get rid of him. Reminiscent of the trickster tales found in many cultures, Bertoldo's simple-mindedness hides a creative and resourceful personality which is quick to face any challenge. In these tales, the underdog takes the day. The listener takes pleasure in hearing how the weak subvert the power of the strong. Time and time again Bertoldo's spirit remains unconquered, always risking his life so that he may live by his code.

Even though one never quite knows what prompts Bertoldo to undermine the king's authority, the listener can't help but be amused by his pranks. According to Elizabeth Mathias and Richard Raspa:

> disobedient characters in Italian folk tales, are often revealed to be clever . . . and praised for their accomplishment though the praise is indirect and paradoxical.[25]

Craftiness, "intelligence and quick wit, when not obviously displayed, are often highly valued"[26] in Italian folklore.

It is this total disregard for social conventions that makes Bertoldo especially fascinating. Through Bertoldo's outrageous acts of rebellion, the listener experiences pure and unadulterated freedom. The trickster is the spirit of disorder, the enemy of boundaries. We are fascinated by him because he represents the principle of pure unbridled energy.[27]

The Bertoldo stories are brought to life each time they are performed. They are social events into themselves which, when shared with others, have the power to transform the mundane routine into a veritable playground of possibilities. One never quite knows what Bertoldo is going to do next, injecting as he does life with suspense and anticipation.

To Graziella the story of Bertoldo evokes fond memories of her grandmother who took care of her after her mother died. In the telling Graziella skillfully performs the part of the king and Bertoldo by modulating her voice for effect. Every so often she breaks into laughter at the audacity of Bertoldo's actions. Through these stories Graziella vicariously experiences a sense of personal autonomy – this, in contrast to a real life scenario that denied her the power to choose a spouse and the freedom to go where she liked without supervision. Under harsh social and economic conditions such stories function as tools for survival. They provide entertainment and release from the burdens of everyday concerns and foster feelings of empowerment and personal control. In this symbolic world, Graziella Di Corpo could be a rabble rouser, turning the world of social convention on its head.

The Mysterious and the Intuitive: Witches, Fortunetellers, Folk Cures and Premonition

In explaining how her husband's side of the family was protected from witchcraft, Anna Del Negro dramatically retold the story of how her husband's grandfather rescued a newborn baby from being sacrificed and returned it safely to the family who had not realized that the child had been kidnapped. At no time during the narration is the authenticity of the story questioned. In fact, my mother validates the story by warning me that things like this do happen. Her belief in witches and supernatural forces is confirmed in stories such as the one in which her sister-in-law Cleonica tested a suspected witch by plunging a knife into the kitchen table and preventing the woman from moving.

When her brother Duillio had been missing

from the war in Abyssinia, now Ethiopia, Anna also remembered how her father was told by a fortuneteller that his son was living as a prisoner of war in a place called Tobruk in Africa. As it turned out, her brother did spend seven years in Africa in a British prison work camp.

Along with the belief in the occult is the practice of traditional folk cures. Special ingredients are believed to have healing power. Immediately after giving birth to her first son, Anna developed a breast infection. At the time her body was producing more milk than her son could consume and, as a result, her nipples became infected. A woman had instructed her to boil a certain type of linen and place it over the nipple. The folk cure, she believed, was effective because the seeds in the linen contained medicinal qualities. What follows are Anna's stories.

Folk Belief

My great grandfather would go to the fair (*fiera*). He left early morning when it was dark. He had walked for two days and near the woods he saw this tiny light very far away. Then he saw two men who had a little baby which they held over the fire. They were witches. So he approached them and asked, "Why are you doing this?" They replied, "This is our work." And he asked, "Where did you take this child from?" They said, "We've taken it from such and such a city." He asked, in a pleading tone, "Give me this child, you are going to let it die." They acquiesced but said, "You must swear not to tell anyone." He swore and returned the baby. He knocked on the door and the mother answered, "Why are you knocking, so early in the morning?" He

told them, "Look near your bed where your baby is."
The lady who was from a noble family with many acres
of land and luxuries went to look and than realized the
baby was missing. "The baby isn't there," my grandfather said. "Well I brought your baby back from the
woods," and so my family has been forever blessed. No
harm could come upon us.

They used to say that my sister-in-law's mother-in-law
was a witch. My sister-in-law, Cleonica, one night went
to visit Aunt Cristina, and it is said that when a witch
comes into your home, you plunge a knife into a table
and they can't move. If you don't remove the knife, the
witch cannot leave. So my sister-in-law said, "Well,
when she comes over to my house, I'll play a joke on
her." So they were talking and she couldn't leave. It was
almost midnight and she was still there. Cleonica felt
sorry for her and removed the knife and she replied,
"Well, I have to leave now." That's what people say. It
still happens!

Folk Cure

When I gave birth I produced a lot of milk. But your
brother Osvaldo didn't suck enough, so my breast got
sick. When the doctor examined, me, he removed this
nasty stuff out. This older lady came to draw my milk
every night and she told me, "What you must do is put
a piece of linen. You boil it and then put it on your nipple and slowly but surely it will get better." In those
days there weren't that many medicines that work mir-
acles like today. This linen contain seeds and they also
make things with it today.

Expressing similar belief in the supernatural, Giuseppina Barbuci reported a prophetic dream she had in
Italy. She foresaw the sewing machine from the fac-

tory where she was later to be employed. Since it was not unusual for an Italian immigrant woman to work in the textile industry, maybe Giuseppina, anticipating her departure, visualized and prepared for the major change that was to occur in her life.

Francesca Mancini's story of "Pianeta," the old man with a fortune telling bird, is also related to the anxieties brought about by immigration. As Francesca describes, the fortuneteller accurately predicted her trip to America.

La Pianeta

One time there was this man who had a parakeet (*pappagallo*) near my house in Italy. The game it played was called *La Pianeta*. The *pappagallo* would take a little piece of paper from the drawer with its beak. There your fortune was written. Well, he told me that I would marry a rich person, that he had a black donkey (*mocha*) and that I would cross the waters to go to America. I paid four cents. They would go from town to town. They carried a box from their neck, and inside the cage was the *pappagallo*. The paper was taken from the little drawer by the *pappagallo* and gave it to the owner and he would read it. I said, "Who is going to bring me to America?" I'm poor, who is going to bring me?" And yet, it's thirty eight years that I'm here.

Although the belief in the supernatural may seem outdated, it continues to persist in the New World. Whether or not one believes in the supernatural, it is important to realize that these women's beliefs are not mere naive fantasy. On the contrary, they evince a faith in the existence of an external reality that directly concerns itself with human destiny, an aspect of the world that cares about human life. Such beliefs help the women to cope with their strange new environment by putting a human face on the often bewildering and random events of urban Canadian life. By retaining their beliefs, they preserve their social identity and develop, in the present, a critical sense of continuity with the past.

Women are often represented in Italian culture as a force to be controlled. Thus, it is not surprising that in Italy, magic, intuition and the natural world are associated with women. By exploiting these associations, women can use magic as an area of female control. Through the *fattura* (a spell frequently cast by women to gain the favor of a suitor), the belief in female second sight and the fear of magical reprisals, women can use the supernatural to their best advantage. In the realm of the magical, women go beyond patriarchy and create a female vision of order and a measure of control over their lives.

As an icon of female power, the witch evokes both fear and awe in men. While magic offers women a sphere of dominion in the symbolic universe of Italian culture, it can also be used against them. While men acknowledge this area of women's power, they also point to magic as evidence that women are force that needs to be controlled. By associating magic with evil and witchcraft with anti-Catholic paganism, women's power is both marginalized and condemned.

Conclusion

It is easy to condemn the unequal treatment of women in traditional Italian society, yet it is important to keep in mind that these beliefs and practices developed in a time of economic scarcity and not one of affluence and choice. In such a context there is little room for personal freedom and growth, at least not according to North American standards. Although, the women interviewed in this study held a subordinate position in the social hierarchy, they were not completely powerless. Despite institutionalized male dominance, the narratives of these nine Italian-Canadian women show how they "used their own creativity and courage to shape, and in some cases escape, the roles presented to them by society."[28]

Economically, the women contributed earnings to the family. Even though for some, going to work outside the home meant betraying traditional beliefs, most of the women worked in factories and found other creative ways of making money, such as working in the black market trade doing piece work at home. For Antonietta De Fronzo, reconciling paid work outside the home with motherhood in the home was difficult and provoked guilt.

Paradoxically, the factory, a place of long hours and low pay, was also the place that offered a sense of personal autonomy. The women who entered the labor market spoke about making many adjustments and compromises, but the atmosphere of amusement (*allegria*) tempered the long work day. Work was a place where women could joke freely. They could even engage in types of behavior which would not be readily acceptable outside the group. The obscene verbal bantering or "mock swearing" connected with work appeared to be a form of occupational lore which helped foster a sense of camaraderie and solidarity among the women.

Contrary to those who found their rights severely shortchanged by arranged marriages, Stefania Annibale found marriage to be a means of achieving respectability and a way of freeing herself from the close scrutiny of the villagers. For those who, because of circumstances and family pressure, had no choice in picking a mate, the rite of passage into womanhood still holds traumatic memories.

An important theme in almost all the interviews was the idea of "being careful." The acute concern with protecting oneself from invisible forces suggested a view of the world as something to be feared. This idea lends itself to various functions. On the one hand, it was a way of assuring mothers that the children would be home promptly; on the other hand, this belief conveyed various cultural messages about what it was like to be a young woman. Although ambiguous, the warnings and stories suggest that women should be diligent at all times because they are easy prey. Intended to elicit feelings of vulnerability, the sayings remind women to "walk the straight path" and are an acceptable way of speaking about sexuality without making explicit references to it. By reinforcing the view of women as potential victims, the patriarchal structure ensures its social and psychological power over women. By defining the dangers and benefits, the rules of behavior and social etiquette of womanhood, folklore is used to teach Italian girls how to become Italian women. Folklore simultaneously teaches those girls to submit to and resist the status quo.

Even within the social and cultural constraints of their society, women developed ways of speaking against, with, through and for the patriarchal structure. Using traditional means of communication, women covertly expressed non traditional messages. Through various folk genres such as folktales, songs and riddles, women engaged in an ongoing symbolic discourse about some of the more value-laden subjects of traditional Italian society – female sexuality, motherhood and personal autonomy. Whether it was by participating in ritual insults at work, talking smart to the opposite sex, drawing upon the powerful imagery of the witch or speaking the unspeakable through song, women found ways of criticizing and subverting the established order.

APPENDIX

Included in this section are stories, jokes, personal experience narratives, folk beliefs and other oral data referred to in the text but not presented in detail. I opted for a near literal translation of the Italian to preserve the spontaneous, expressive aspects of the Italian language. These passages are also accented with words borrowed from the colorful Italian-Canadian vocabulary.[1] I also have tried to capture the unique sounds of the women's regional dialects in my spelling, especially if it is crucial to the rhyme or meter of the song.

Giuseppina Barbuci

Average Families

If I wanted to visit another town, I would go. I would take my bike from town to town. My parents never forbade me not to go places. I never felt subordinate, no never. Most families were like that. You had a few families who were very strict, but they were the wealthy families, who thought they were special. I always mixed company with average families . . . I've always been tough during my youth. You know in our region we used to thresh wheat; both men and women. . . . I was

never afraid of anyone, there were women who didn't
want to go . . . In the village we used to give dogs injec-
tions. One day there was a beautiful young man who
came by. He kept hanging around, but I was uninterest-
ed in him because he was rich. I thought to myself:
"He's trying to take me for a ride. He wants to amuse
himself." He was of a different social class. Every time
he would come by he would tell me nasty words. I did-
n't want to know him from Adam. One day I saw him
on my path to get water. He was giving a dog an injec-
tion and to tease me he began to bark, making the dog
bark too. I took a rock and it landed on his knee. I gave
him a big bruise. He said to me, "Look how bad you
are" and he asked "Why did you do that?" "Because," I
told him, "next time you'll let the dog stay in its place
or play with your sister." The same day we were thresh-
ing. I like to be on the tractor. In a lot of villages you
wouldn't [dream] of seeing a woman on machines. So
one day this very same young man came by . . . It was a
beautiful hot summer day in the month of July. We
would sun bathe and talk. So he passes by and knocks
on the machine from the back. I had seen him. I took a
fork stick and I hit him on the arm. He couldn't work
that day, because of his swollen arm. His sister told me,
"You've got it in for my brother" – and I said, "He has
it in for me. If he minded his own business things would
be fine." He was a few years older then me. He liked to
pinch me (*pizzicatta*).

Community Work

Sometimes it's too much, but fortunately, thank the
lord, I've got a lot of experience. I learned a lot because
if I'd have stayed home I wouldn't know what I know.
Okay, I work a lot. I run here, run there. Even if it isn't
a lot of work, there is a great deal of thinking and plan-

ning. I also have a lot to do for my family. You're gone
one day here, one day there. But I am grateful for my
husband, because if I had a husband who said, "You
can't go there or here," I would have stayed home.
That's why I respect my husband for where I am today,
because it's also partly his doing. He could have told me
not to go places. I would have felt bad, now I know
both places [Centro Donne and home], and they're
close to my heart.

Feisty Peasant Girl

So I was always strong always! If someone approached
me nicely, someone with a nice way it would go well.
My sister was never like this. She was nicer, sometimes
she couldn't defend herself.

Germans

During the war we watched out for the Germans. When
they came they would steal everything we had. One
time they came with machine guns into our bedrooms.
We had a whole bunch of people in there. They came
with their guns looking for men, but the men were hiding. We weren't the ones they wanted to talk to. One of
my cousins said, "They have no business being here."
"We're all young girls here" [*raising her voice and laughing*] When they heard that they pointed the gun right at
her. They didn't shoot, but they certainly gave us a
scare.

The Horns

I am happy with my husband. We understand each
other. He isn't jealous . . . It's not as if he says to me,
"You can't do this," I do what I want. I respect him, I
think that if I had a husband who watched my every

move, I think I might have either left him or cuckolded him (*messo le corna*). If you don't have a choice.

Joke

I remember a funny joke. There was a young man who went to visit his fiancée. They were to marry soon. His fiancée was a little richer. This man didn't have a suit to go to his girlfriend's house to meet her parents. This man's parents told him, "Well, you have your suit from your first communion." Back then people had their communion when they were older. So the suit wasn't that small, but it also wasn't big enough. He put his suit on and off he went. The suit was tight-tight-tight: he could barely walk in it. He walked a little and tore the seat of his pants. When he arrived at his girlfriend's place they gave him a chair with a hole in the seat. He sat down to speak with his future father-in-law who said to him, "I give my daughter the dowry. You, what do you have?" He said, "Well, I live with my parents. I have my parents' small house." You see there was this cat who all along had been playing underneath the chair [*laughs*]. He resisted. The father kept asking, "Well what do you own? what do you have? He finally got mad and got up from the chair and said will you give me your daughter's hand before the cat eats *the little that I do own*" [*laughs*].

Nine Canadian Soldiers

After the war we harbored nine Canadian soldiers at our house. There was one of the soldiers who wanted to marry my sister who was fifteen years old. The soldier had given her a ring and told her that, "Once the war was over I will come back for you." There was also an

Italian-Canadian among them. When they were at our
house they ate spaghetti. The laughs we used to have.
They didn't know how to eat spaghetti. I remember this
almost as if it was today . . . In one room there were several bunk beds and my mother cooked to feed them all.
They used to hide in the basement in the day and at
night they would come up to eat . . . They cried when
they left.

Suitors

I wanted a family of my own, a nice home. I had lived
in Italy for a good part of my adolescence. It's not as if
I came here as young [greenhorn]. I had been engaged.
I had other suitors. I always kept an eye out for those
who spoke well – good prospects. Those whom I knew
were not good for me I would let pass. In my village
there was a young man who didn't live far from my
house. He was crazy for me. But he never got along
with his mother. I couldn't stand him for this. But you
know he would have killed for me. But the fact that he
didn't like his mother bothered me. I thought to myself,
"Today he says these words to his mother, tomorrow it
will be me." Even when I left my fiancé it hurt me, but
before marrying I thought of many things. Here it is difficult because you don't know the family. But in the
small towns you know everyone and everything. So it's
easier to know the good path, the bad path *(la strada
diritta e la strada cattiva)* . . . When I married my husband I didn't know his family but his family lived close
by so I occasionally got to speak to his mother and
father. It was difficult to make up my mind. You always
find a defect. I wasn't perfect either, but that's the way
I was. Nobody could change me. What do you want to
do? Anyway, even before coming here I didn't want a
rich boy. I thought of marrying a well-mannered boy. I

liked someone who held doors, held your hand. Even if he was gruff in other aspects, as long as he had these qualities. My husband did these things at the beginning but he doesn't do them anymore.

Work

The first few days at work were difficult. I wasn't used to staying seated for eight hours. That was the hardest part. Staying seated for that long and then the work. I wasn't used to doing piece work. I used to baste the collars of men's jackets. I had a female boss, and she was not too nice, not too bad. I earned forty-five cents an hour! I didn't find the work particularly difficult because in Italy sometimes we used to work harder than here. It was difficult to stay put for eight hours a day. My behind got sore from sitting. Then I got used to it. I liked the company. We were always in good spirits (*allegre*). We used to sing, joke, the boss couldn't really tell us anything because we're doing piece work. I wasn't frustrated like some women. I personally didn't experience that.

Antonietta De Fronzo

Cardellino

Questa mattina nel mio giardino c'era un picollo uccello.
Era un picollo uccellino.
Era carino.
Suo nome era Cardellino.
Per cantar diceva ci, ci, ci, ci, ci,
Per volare così,
Così.

Un giorno un cacciatore. . . scoppiò e pa.
Il povero uccellino cadò per terra.

(This morning in my small garden was a small bird.
He was a small birdie.
He was a small cutie.
His name was Cardellino.
To sing he would say ci, ci, ci, ci, ci, ci,
To fly like this,
Like this [*waving her arms in flying motion and laughing*].
One day a mean hunter. . . as it burst it went boom.
The poor birdie fell to the ground.)

The Chestnut (Il cecce)

We use to get around the fire, because we didn't have any heating, before we used a brazier (*fuoco del braciere*). We put wood chips, some carbon and fire and we would gather round, and my mother would tell us well if you stay quiet I'll tell you a story . . . She used to say often, so there was a little girl, she was ill. There was a scary old man who asked, "Please give me a chestnut, I need a chestnut (*cecce*)," and he told her, "Well, you either give the *cecce* or you give me your daughter who is sick." And the mother takes the chestnut and gives it to him [and says]: "But the daughter, no." And he went from home to home and he would say, "Or I take the *cecce* or I'll take the chicken" [*laughs*], until he put everything in a bag. And then he went to another house and said, "Give me the two children." My mother would try to scare us. He would say, "Or give me two children and I'll give you this bag – let's swap," and she said, "No." Anyway, she was forced to give her two children. We used to get so scared. So he put his children on his shoulders, in the bags, and these children were crying in the bag. He was taking them away to who knows where. So to one he cut his nose to the other his ear [*laughs*]. We used to get so scared and my mother would say, "You see you mustn't go out, if someone comes to open the door, see what they do" [*laughs*]. And then the mother called the police and went to this man and they said that this man was alone, and he didn't have any children. He started wanting the chestnut and ended up wanting the children; and then he didn't have any food left, so he began by cutting off the nose of one and the ear of the other. These were stories to scare us.

The Clock

Stamattina l'orologio dice:
Bambini fate presto,
Presto piccoli,
Che l'ora è arrivata,
Tic e Tic,
Tic e Toc.
Tic e Tic,
Tic e To.
Quando viene la sera,
i bambini vanno a casa,
Dove la mamma aspetta.
Dove si va per riposare,
Tic e tac,
Tic e tac.

(This morning the clock says:
Children be quick,
Quick little ones.
That the time has come,
Tic and Tic,
Tic and Toc.
Tic and Tic,
Tic and To.

When night comes,
The children go home.
Where mommy is waiting,
They go to rest.
Tic and Tac,
Tic and Tac.)

Maria, Maria

C'era qualcuno che si chiamava Maria, Maria,
sto sul primo scalino.
Maria, Maria, sto sul secondo scalino.
Maria, Maria, sto sul terzo scalino.
Maria, Maria, sto dietro la porta.
Maria, Maria, sto per venire dentro.

(There was someone called . . . Maria, Maria,
I'm at the first step.
Maria, Maria, I'm on the second step.
Maria, Maria, I'm on the third step.
Maria, Maria, I'm in the back of the door.
Maria, Maria, I'm about to come inside.)

Anna Del Negro

Butcher Shop Ritual

I used to sing when I would help my father butcher animals at the slaughterhouse. We prepared many things –
clean *la trippa* (tripe, intestines), blood (*sangue*). We
had a chimney to cook the blood. The blood would
boil, we would slaughter the goats and we would put
the blood in a container and it became hard. We would
put the blood in boiling water and it would turn into a

hard consistent blood, like a small salami (*salamino*), like a Polish sausage, with blood inside. I couldn't tell you what it's called. Even in Belgium they used to do this – put the blood in the intestines with spices and everything. My father would sell it in pieces to peasants (*contadini*), poor people who could not buy meat.

Community

People cared and paid attention to me because I didn't have my mother. Then friends and our small town of three thousand inhabitants we all knew each other – doctors, butchers, pharmacist, policeman. Everyone knew each other, there wasn't any partiality, when we met in the streets good morning (*buon giorno*), goodbye (*arrivederci*). We would chat, we weren't in a hurry like here in America. There, life was nice. We worked hard, but there wasn't any stress. There was calm.

The Crying Maiden
(La bella che piangeva)

My father used to sing this to me. He had been in the 1914-18 war:

Camminando per Milano una notte di pioggia.
La bella che piangeva,
la bella che piangeva con il fazzoletto in mano.
Con fazzoletto in mano,
si asciugò le lacrime guardando il giovane
ragazzo partire per la guerra
partir per la guerra.
Guardandolo cadere,
guardandolo cadere da una ferita al cuor,
Una ferita al cuor ed un altra alla vita.

Oh mamma, sono stata tradita,
Oh mamma, sono stata tradita.
Tradita dall amor, tradita dall amor, tradita dagli amici.
Oh mamma, sono ferita,
Oh mamma, sono ferita dall amor.

(Walking by Milan on a rainy evening.
The maiden was crying,
The maiden was crying with handkerchief in hand.
With handkerchief in hand,
She dried her eyes watching the young man
leave to be a soldier,
Leave to be a soldier for war.
And watching him fall,
Watching him fall from a wound at the heart,
A wound at the heart and another to his life.
Oh mamma, I've been betrayed,
Oh mamma, I've been betrayed.
Betrayed by love, betrayed by love,
betrayed by my friends.
Oh mamma, I'm wounded,
Oh mamma, I'm wounded by love . . .)

Sleep, Sleep
(Dormi, dormi)

Dormi, dormi, picollo bambino,
Mentre veglia su di te.
Sogni, picollo amore,
che sta accanto al mio cuor.

(Sleep, sleep little one.
While I watch over you.
Dream small love
close to my heart . . .)

Fountain of Carpineto
(La fonte di Carpineto)

Now I will sing a song about my town, Carpineto-Sinello (Abruzzo):

È la fonte di Carpinete, la riulette, e la riulaie,
è la fonte di Carpinete a otto cannelle . . .
e ca la liggire li voie, la riulette, e la riulaie,
e ca la liggire li voie la moia bella . . .

È la moia bella a chi, la riulette, e la riulaie
è la moia bella a chi li sa tineie . . .
È la terra bona a chi, la riulette, e la riulaie,
è la terra bona a chi, li sa zappaie . . .

È li quatrina a chi, la riulette, e la riulaie,
è li quatrina a chi li sa cuntaie . . .

È chi ti la ditte ca, la riulette, e la riulaie,
chi ti la ditte ca lu prete è bone . . . e lu prete è lu cape,

la riulette, e la riulaie, lu prete è lu cape lazzarone...
E chi ti la ditte ca, la riulette, e la riulaie,
chi ti la ditte ca lu prete è sante. . . e lu prete è lucape,
la riulette, e la riulaie, lu prete è lu cape di li brigante.. .

(It's the fountain of Carpineto,
la riulette, la riulaie [refrain],
It's the fountain of Carpineto with eight taps . . .
and I turn and turn the problems,
la riulette, e la riulaie,
and that I turn and turn problems,
I want a pretty wife.

And the pretty wife to who *la riulette, e la riulaie,*
And the pretty wife for who can keep her. . .

It's the good earth to who, *la riulette, e la riulaie,*
It's the good earth to he who knows how to till the soil.

And it's the money to who, *la riulette, e la riulaie,*
And it's the money to he who knows how to count.

And who told you that, *la riulette, e la riulaie,*
Who told you that the priest is good . . .

the priest is the head, *la riulette, e la riulaie,*
the priest is a rascal . . .

And who told you that, *la riulette, e la riulaie,*
Who told you that the priest is a saint . . .
the priest is the head, *la riulette, e la riulaie,*
the priest is the head of the thieves.)

We sang when we swept, went to get water at the well. You would take a dishcloth and make a cloth base (*una spara*). [In Italy, women place water buckets on their heads when carrying water back from the well. They use the *spara* to balance the bucket on their heads while walking.] You roll it up and then tuck it in on one side. You put in on your head, place the bucket on it and then go get water. We didn't have running water back then, we didn't have bathrooms for that matter. We used to go to the *stalla* (barns) where the animals were, but you could be clean.

Maestra Pestone

There was a teacher I liked a lot, her name was Maestra Pestone . . . I remember one day I had gone early in the morning to pick up nuts that we fed the sheep (*la glan-ulla*). Then I went to school and my teacher asked me to recite a poem about the autumn. All I could come up with was, "The leaves are falling [*laughs*], the fall is coming," and that's all I kept repeating. Then the teacher said, "Anna, what's in your head today?" I said, "I don't know, I'm very tired all I can remember is the leaves are falling." Then I started to laugh and told her, "Well, this is all I could do for today," and she told me, "Okay, it's fine for today we'll take it up another time" [*laughs*].

Nell', Nell'
Nell', Nell', Nell',
Cuant' è bella lu gitela me.
Nell', Nell', Nell',
Cuant' sa dorme stu gitela me.
Ninna nanna, ninna nanna,
ninna nanna . . .

(Nell', Nell', Nell'
This nice child is so nice.
Nell', Nell', Nell'
When is my baby going to sleep.
Ninna nanna, ninna nanna,
ninna nanna . . .)

Riverito

We would get up early, eat at noon and then go for a siesta. But I went to the seamstress from 1:00 to 5:00 for three years, then finished and I learned to cut. I liked it a lot. The teacher was very nice. She was a good teacher. We used to call her Maestra and we had to respect her. I was stubborn; I didn't want say "riverisca" (the formal greeting). In Italy in the morning we say good day ("*buon giorno*"), and in the afternoon we say "*riverito*," and in the evening good evening ("*buona sera*"). Since she and I were friends I didn't want to say "*riverito*." This word was very difficult for me. This lady was a friend of the family, so I didn't feel obligated. So the teacher, not because she was mean, one day decided to teach me a lesson. One day she told me, "Listen, tomorrow you're going to say *riverito*," The day after, I was so stubborn, I didn't say anything and the second day I went to her house and she kicked me out and told me, "When you'll have the courage to say *riverito* you shall enter." I didn't want to go home because my mother wasn't home, my sister would have licked me but good – the whippings would make smoke (*le bastonate facevano il fumo*) so I returned and said "*riverito*." From that day forward I said "*riverito*," but that first step was like having been sentenced to death. I was shy and also proud.

Genoveffa Della Zazzera

Community

Life was serene, tranquil. There wasn't anything. There was poverty, but there was peace; there was tranquility. You didn't hear of terrible things like today, there wasn't any radio, television, gramophone nothing . . . my father played the guitar, and then there was a feast. He played the guitar, mandolin, violin and harmonica.

Song

Ti voglio baciar,
ti voglio baciar,
però il mio cuor dice. . .
Ti voglio . . .

(I would like to kiss you,
I would like to kiss you,
but my heart tells . . .
I want you . . .)

Francesca Mancini

I didn't find any snow . . . but a biting cold. In fact one
night I came home, it was so cold, we had a small room
and I found two or three people with my husband. They
were chatting, sitting near the heater. I pulled a joke on
them. I said, "Oh, look how it's snowing outside." They
got up and I made myself comfortable near the heater
[*laugh*].

Obscene Bantering

We used to work at a table where they did the finishing
(*le finisce*, an Italianization of the English verb, "to fin-
ish"). The table was the table of fun (*allegria*). All Italians. At noon everyone came to our table to listen to
Italian jokes. . . they were dirty, we would say riddles,
jokes.
Insult Word Play: Kill you and your mother, and you,
your mother and you . . . go get lost. ("*Accise a tu
mamme, e tu, tu mammete e tu . . . vatt'a fa fotte.*"
[*Accise* is a homophone with the english word "cheese"
and here is used as a pun.])

Ritual Insults

At work there were English people who also spoke Italian. One time a woman wanted to pass her work for the
finishing on a jacket. The other women shouted,
"Francesca, sew the button, sew the button" [*teasing
tone*]. She would say, "Have you finished damn

(*cazzo*)." [The word *cazzo* is a curse word in Italian; it is best translated as a combination of the English curses "damn", "fuck" or "shit."] One day [*laughs*], the boss who spoke Italian, Famme, was behind a column and he heard someone say, Have you finished, you fuck? ("*L'hai finita cazzo?*") This was noon time, and he popped in to look and he said, "Signora Mancini, you don't say that word" [*laughs*]. We talked about everything. For instance – when we arrived here in Canada, the children in Italy, food. Then the boss of the factory gave us permission to bring an espresso machine to make coffee. He even took the first cup. We used to take it three times a day. All very nice people; sometimes we used to fight [*laughs*].

The Time the Germans Came

We were eighteen people with my husband's family. We all slept in the same room. During the day we'd go hide for fear of the Germans. One day on the eighteenth of November 1943 the Germans came to the countryside (*la campagna*). They turned the house upside down. That day we had baked bread. We were at home; there was me and my three children, and my sister-in-law, the teacher; and inside the water bucket (*conca*) they found a strip of ammunition. They took us outside and said, "You partisan (*partigiani*), *caput*, *caput*," so they put us near an olive tree, tied up all four of us. My sister-in-law, the teacher said, "Or I save the whole bunch or we die." She spoke French with them and we were saved.

NOTES

Chapter One

1. Frances de Caro, *Women and Folklore: A Bibliographic Survey* (West Port, Connecticut: Greenwood Press, 1983).

2. Danielle Lee-Juteau and Barbara Roberts, "Ethnicity and femininity: d'après nos experiences," *Canadian Ethnic Studies* 8, no. 1 (1981), 5.

3. Ann Cornelisan, *Women of the Shadows: A Study of Wives and Mothers of Southern Italy* (New York: Vintage Books, 1976).

4. Loaded with derogatory implications, the word *miseria* has often been used to invoke the stereotype of Italians as rural, backward people who live in a world where only the devious and cunning survive. Despite the negative connotations, this term was retained for two reasons. First, it is the word that was most frequently used to describe the devastation Italians experienced after World War II. Second, it is the word the women repeatedly used to convey the despair that led them to seek asylum in another land.

5. Barbara Babcock, "Taking Liberties, Writing from the Margins, and Doing It with a Difference." *Journal of American Folklore* 100 (1987), 390-411.

6. This phrase was coined by Barbara Kirshenblatt-Gimblett in "The Future of Folklore Studies in America: The Urban Frontier," *Folklore Forum* 16 (1983), 175.

7. For a discussion of similar ideas about folklore see Henry Glassie, *The Spirit of Folk Art* (New York: Abrams, 1989; Sante Fe, New Mexico: Museum of International Folk Art, 1989.)

8. See Claire Farrer, ed., *Women and Folklore: Images and Genres* (Prospect Heights, Illinois: Waveland Press, 1975), 14; Susan K. Webster, "Women and Folklore: Performers, Characters, Scholars," *Women's Studies International Forum* 9 (1986), 219-226.

9. Claire Farrer, ed., *Women and Folklore, 14. Since this study, the notions of public and private spheres have begun to undergo scholarly reevaluation. See Rosemary J. Coombe, "Barren Ground: Re-Conceiving Honour and Shame in the Field of Mediterranean Ethnography," Anthropologia* 32 (1990), 221-238; Jill Dubisch, ed., *Gender and Power in Rural Greece* (Princeton, New Jersey: Princeton University Press, 1986); Michael Herzfeld, "Silence, Submission, and Subversion: Toward a

Poetics of Womanhood,"in *Contested Identities*, eds. Peter Loisos and Evthymios Papataxiarchis (New Jersey: Princeton University Press, 1991), 79-97; Michael Herzfeld, "Within and Without: The Category of "Female" in the Ethnography of Modern Greece', in *Gender and Power in Rural Greece*, ed. Jill Dubisch, 215-233; Evthymios Papataxiarchis and Peter Loizes, *Contested Identities: Gender and Kinship in Modern Greece* (Princeton, New Jersey: Princeton University Press, 1991).

10. Danielle Lee-Juteau and Barbara Roberts, "Ethnicity and Femininity," 6.

11. See Joan N. Radner and Susan S. Lanser in "The Feminist Voice: Strategies of Coding in Folklore and Literature," *Journal of American Folklore* 100 (1987), 58-85.

12. Alessandro Falassi, *Folklore by the Fireside: Text and Context of the Tuscan Veglia* (Austin: University of Texas Press, 1980), 156.

13. The word "tradition" in folklore has undergone massive analytical scrutiny making its meaning somewhat tenuous. I use "traditional" to describe the shared experiences of a group of women. That is not to say that all women from the regions and classes of Italy responded to their culture in similar ways; however, the Italian immigrant women I interviewed reveal in their testimonies a cultural system that greatly influenced, but did not determine, their behavior.

14. Emiliana Noether, "The Silent Half: *Le Contadine del sud* before the First World War," in *The Italian Immigrant Women in North America*, eds. Betty Boyd Caroli, Robert Harney and Lydio Tomassi (Toronto: Multicultural History Society of Ontario, 1978), 8.

15. C. L. Johnson, "The Maternal Role in Contemporary Italian-American Family," in *The Italian Immigrant Woman in North America*, eds. Betty Boyd Caroli, Robert Harney and Lydio Tomassi, 237.

16. Vincenza Scarpaci, "Contadina: Plaything of the Middle Class Woman Historian," *Ethnic Studies* 9 (1981), 21-38.

17. Betty Boyd Caroli, "Introduction," in *The Italian Immigrant Woman in North America*, eds. Betty Boyd Caroli, Robert Harney and Lydio Tomassi, 7.

18. Franca Iacovetta, "Trying to Make Ends Meet: An Historical Look at Italian-Canadian Women: The State and Family Survival Strategies in Post War Toronto," *Canadian Women's Studies: Cahiers de la femme* 8, no. 2 (1987), 10.

19. Ibid., 11.

20. Herbert Gans, *The Urban Villagers: Group and Class in the Life of Italian Americans* (New York: Free Press, 1962).

21. Tuilio Tentori, "Social Classes in Matera," in *Mediterranean Family Structures*, ed. John Peristiany (New York: Cambridge Press, 1976), 278.

22. Ibid., 278.

23. Ann Cornelisan, *Women of the Shadows*.

24. Tuilio Tentori, "Social Classes in Matera," 278.

25. Ibid., 278.

26. Ibid., 278.

27. Ibid., 278.

28. Leo Cellini, "Emigration, the Italian Family and Changing Roles," in *The Italian Immigrant Woman in North America*, eds. Betty Boyd Caroli, Robert Harney and Lydio Tomassi, 273-278.

29. Herbert Gans, *The Urban Villagers,* 50.

30. Ibid., 48.

31. Richard Gambino, *Blood of My Blood: The Dilemma of the Italian-Americans* (New York: Doubleday, 1974; rpt. Toronto/New York: Guernica, 1996); Valentine Rosseli Winsey, "The Italian Immigrant Women Who Arrived in the United States Before World War I," in *Studies in Italian American Social History*, ed. Francesco Cordasco (Towtawa, New Jersey: Rowan & Littlefield, 1975), 199-210; Franca Iacovetta, "Trying to Make Ends Meet," 6-11.

32. Emiliana Noether, "The Silent Half: *Le contadine del sud* before the First World War," in *The Italian Immigrant Woman in North America*, eds. Betty Boyd Caroli, Robert Harney and Lydio Tomassi, 49.

33. John Peristiany, *Honour and Shame: The Values of Mediterranean Society* (Chicago: University of Chicago Press, 1966). During the course of my research on the construction of gender and sexuality in central Italy, I have become acquainted with the growing literature that challenges earlier notions of honor and shame in Mediterranean society. See Rosemary J. Coombe, "Barren Ground: Re-Conceiving Honour and Shame In the Field of Mediterranean Ethnography," *Anthropologia* 32 (1990), 221-238; Jill Dubisch, ed., *Gender and Power in Rural Greece*; Michael Herzfeld, "Silence, Submission, and Subversion: Toward a Poetics of Womanhood," 79-97; Michael Herzfeld, "Within and Without: The Category of "Female" in the Ethnography of Modern Greece," 215-233; Peter Loizses and Evthymios Papataxiarchis, *Contested Identities*.

34. John Peristiany, *Honour and Shame*.

35. Harriet Perry, "The Metonymic Definition of the Female and the Concept of Honour Among Italian Immigrant Families in Toronto," in *The Italian Immigrant Woman in North America*, eds. Betty Boyd Caroli, Robert Harney and Lydio Tomassi, 229.

36. Barbara Myerhoff, *Number Our Days* (New York: Simon and Schuster, 1978); Jeff Titon, "The Life Story," *Journal of American Folklore* 93 (1980), 276-292; Sandra K. Dolby-Stahl, "A Literary Folkloristic: Methodology for the Study of Meaning in Personal Narrative," *Journal of Folklore Research* 22 (1985), 45-69.

37. Italian oral historian Luisa Passerini makes a similar point in her impressive study of the effects of fascism on the working class of Turin, *Fascism in Popular Memory* (New York: Cambridge University Press, 1987). According to her, narrative forms borrow from the culture's folk repertoire of stories. Passerini explains "when someone is asked for his life-story, his memory draws upon pre-existing story-lines of telling stories, even if these are in part modified" (8).

38. Linda Degh, *People in the Tobacco Belt: Four Lives* (Ottawa, Ontario: National Museum of Canada, 1972), 78.

39. Waletzy and Labov as quoted in John A. Robinson, "Personal Narrative Reconsidered," *Journal of American Folklore* 94 (1981), 58-85. These scholars highlight the ego-gratifying benefits for the narrator while others stress the didactic functions.

40. Linda Degh, *People in the Tobacco Belt;* John A. Robinson, "Personal Narrative Reconsidered," *Journal of American Folklore* 94 (1981), 58-85.

41. Giovanna P.Del Negro, "'So I was always strong, always': The Rebellious Self-Image in the Personal Narrative of Italian-Canadian Women." Unpublished research paper prepared for independent study with Prof. Sandra Dolby-Stahl, Folklore Institute, Indiana University, 1991.

42. Sandra Dolby-Stahl, *Literary Folkloristics and the Personal Narrative* (Bloomington: Indiana University, 1989), 25.

43. Richard Bauman, *Verbal Art as Performance* (Prospect Heights, Illinois: Waveland Press, 1977); John A. Robinson, "Personal Narrative Reconsidered," 64.

44. See the discussion of Goffman in John Robinson, "Personal Narrative Reconsidered," 58-85. See also Alessandro Portelli, *The Death of Luigi Trastulli and Other Stories: Form and Meaning in Oral History* (Albany: State University of New York Press, 1991). Portelli's work underscores the subjectivity of memory and describes how people use various rhetorical strategies to organize and relate the past. Portelli argues that oral histories invariably depart from an objective, linear chronological understanding of the past. Citing William Labov he states that "a story is told naturally not when it adheres to objective chronology, but when it departs from it in order to incorporate subjective meaning." Portelli, 253.

45. Susan Kalcik and Rosan Ann Jordan, eds., *Women's Folklore, Women's Culture* (Philadelphia: University of Pennsylvania Press, 1985); Barbara Myerhoff, *Number Our Days* (New York: Simon and Schuster, 1978). For an excellent and recent publication on oral history scholarship I strongly recommend, Sherna Berger Gluck and Dahpne Patai's *Women's Words: The Feminist Practice of Oral History* (New York: Routledge

Press, 1991). This book provides a critique of traditional oral history methodology and discusses exciting new feminist approaches to the topic.

46. Susan Kalcik, " '. . . like Anne's gynecologist or the time I was almost raped': Personal Narratives in Women's Rap Groups," in *Women and Folklore: Images and Genres*, ed. Claire Farrer, 6.

47. See Kristina Minster's article, "A Feminist Frame of the Oral History Interview," in *Women's Words: The Feminist Practice of Oral History* (New York: Routledge Press, 1991).

48. In a telephone conversation about this incident, anthropology professor Donna Budani suggested that the woman who prodded me with this pointed question was indirectly trying to gauge my character and trustworthiness. By cutting to the chase and asking such an unexpected question my response became a litmus test of my character (Personal Communication, Donna Coppola-Budani, Oct 25, 1992.)

In "The Postmodernist Turn in Anthropology: Cautions From a Feminist Perspective," *Signs* 15 (1989), 7-33, Frances E. Mascia-Lees, Patricia Sharpe and Colleen Ballerino Cohen shed additional light on this topic. There, quoting and expounding upon Judith Stacey, they argue that "the highly personalized relationship between ethnographer and research subject, which masks actual differences in power, knowledge, and structural mobility, places research subjects at grave risk of manipulation and betrayal by the ethnographer." Judith Stacey, "Can There Be a Feminist Ethnography?" in *Women's Studies International Forum* 11, no.1 (1988), 21-27, esp, 22-23' Mascia-Lees, Sharpe and Cohen, 21. Alessandro Portelli, in *The Death of Luigi Trastulli*, also points out that the researcher is studied by the people she/he works with as much as she/he studies them.

Chapter Two

1. "Women's Personal Narratives: Myths, Experience and Emotions," in *Interpreting Women's Lives: Feminist Theory and Personal Narratives*, ed. Personal Narrative Group (Bloomington: Indiana Press, 1989), 189.

2. These stories also were intended to prepare young women to face the dangerous forces that lurk in the outside world. In a sense, these cautionary tales are a training ground for young women, daring them to be strong and teaching them to be unaffected by potentially harmful external forces. (I gratefully acknowledge Donna Coppola-Budani's help in developing this idea.)

3. Narratives are located in the *Appendix* and referred to by the teller's name and the title of the narrative.

4. Richard Gambino, *Blood of My Blood*.

5. Herbert Gans, *The Urban Villagers*.

6. Roger Abrahams, "Negotiating Respect: Patterns of Presentation Among Black Women," in *Women and Folklore: Images and Genres*, ed Claire Farrer, 58-80.

7. Food and plentifulness were very important to my family. The word *abbondanza* invokes images of the hearth, love and warmth. Of course plentifulness also said economic security; this was especially significant to my parents' generation who clearly remember the scarcity and privation of their youth.

8. For an interesting study of the role of the *veglia* (storytelling gathering) in Tuscany, see Alessandro Falassi, *Folklore by the Fireside: Text and Context of the Tuscan Veglia* (Austin: University of Texas Press, 1980).

9. Since our last interview Mrs. Lorenzo lost her battle with throat cancer.

10. Bernice Martin, *Sociology of Contemporary Cultural Change* (New York: St. Martin's Press, 1981).

11. One event particularly stands out in my mind. While my father and I watched the evening news one night, he started to reminisce about the experiences of his youth – how he survived the war and later saved the lives of his friends in a mining disaster. This was my fathers way of telling me that he too was part of history and that his story should be told. I don't know if it was out of a sense of guilt, but I told him that I would record his stories as soon as I could. Time has past, and, unfortunately, I have yet to interview him.

12. Lawrence W. Levine, *Black Culture and Black Consciousness* (New York: Oxford Press, 1978), 41.

Chapter Three

1. These practices, although common, were not uniformly enforced by all families; regional and class differences apply.

2. Richard Gambino, *Blood of My Blood*; Herbert Gans, *The Urban Villagers*; Tuilio Tentori, "Social Classes in Matera," in *Mediterranean Family Structures*, ed. John Peristiany (New York: Cambridge Press, 1976); Franca Iacovetta, "Trying to Make Ends Meet," 6-11.

3. Franca Iacovetta, "Trying to Make Ends Meet," 7.

4. Inez Freeman-Cardozo, "Games Mexican Girls Play," in *Women and Folklore*, ed. Claire Farrer (Prospects Heights, Illinois: Waveland Press, 1983), 13.

5. Franca Iacovetta, "Trying to Make Ends Meet," 7.

6. Ibid.

7. Ibid.

8. Ibid.

9. These stories, as I mentioned in first chapter, are a training ground of sorts; they challenge women to be strong and resolute in the face of potentially harmful external forces. At the same time, however, they also help rationalize the forced seclusion of women.

10. Alessandro Falassi, *Folklore by the Fireside,* 44.

11. Ibid.

12. Peter Burke, *Popular Culture in Early Modern Europe* (New York: New York University Press, 1978).

13. Alessandro Falassi, *Folklore by the Fireside*.

14. I would like to thank Harris M. Berger for his keen observations on this topic. Our conversations helped me to foreground an idea which I had not elaborated upon in my thesis.

15. Bess Lomax Hawes, "Folksongs and Functions: Some Thoughts on the American Lullaby," *Journal of American Folklore* 87 (1974), 71.

16. This nonsense syllable is related to the Italian word *ninna nanna* (lullaby) and serves a similar function to "fa, la, la" in English language songs.

17. Bess Lomax Hawes, "Folksongs and Functions," 66-71.

18. Joan N. Radner and Susan S. Lanser, "The Feminist Voice: Strategies of Coding in Folklore and Literature," *Journal of American Folklore* 100 (1987), 412-425.

19. Alessandro Falassi, *Folklore by the Fireside*; Joan Radner and Susan Lanser, "The Feminist Voice," 412-425.

20. Barbara Babcock, *The Reversible World: Symbolic Inversion in Art and Society* (New York: Cornell Press, 1978), 29.

21. Alessandro Falassi, *Folklore by the Fireside*, 90.

22. Ibid., 80.

23. Jan Brunvand, *The Study of American Folklore: An Introduction*, 2nd ed., (New York: W.W. Norton Company, 1978), 67.

24. Alessandro Falassi, *Folklore by the Fireside*, 90.

25. Elizabeth Mathias and Richard Raspa, *Italian Folktales in America: The Verbal Art of an Immigrant Woman* (Detroit: Wayne State University Press, 1978).

26. Ibid., 11.

27. Roger D. Abrahams, "Trickster: The Outrageous Hero," in *Oral Tradition*, ed. Tristram P. Coffin (New York: Basic Books, 1968); Tristram P. Coffin, and Hennig Cohen, *Folklore in America* (New York: Doubleday, 1966), 170.

28. Elaine Jahner, "Women Remembering Life History as Exemplary Pattern," in *Women's Folklore, Women's Culture*, eds. Susan Kalcik and Rosan Ann Jordan, 214.

Appendix

1. Italians in Montreal frequently mix standard Italian with regional dialects and occasionally use loan words from English or French. They also "Italianize" English words like, *lo bosso*, taken from the English, boss. An informal survey in Montreal included such words as *blocco, baga, ceca, cotto, ghirla, gudbai* and *turna* (block, bag, cake, coat, girl, good bye and turn). The use of code-switching is yet another way of accommodating Italian to the English and French language. Yole Correa-Zoli describes how "frequent interjections, for some individuals almost mannerism, displays various degrees of phonetic, adaptation, such as *aino, orriate, sciuro, etzol* (I know, all right, sure, that's all)." From "The Language of Italian-Americans," in *Language in the USA*, ed. Charles Ferguson and Shirley Brice Heath (Cambridge: Cambridge University Press, 1981), 247.

BIBLIOGRAPHY

Abrahams, Roger D. "Trickster: The Outrageous Hero." In *Oral Tradition*, ed. Tristram P. Coffin. New York: Basic Books, 1968.

Abrahams, Roger D. "Negotiating Respect: Patterns of Presentation among Black Women." In *Women and Folklore*, ed. Claire Farrer. Prospects Heights, Illinois: Waveland Press, 1975, 58-81.

Babcock, Barbara. *The Reversible World: Symbolic Inversion in Art and Society*. New York: Cornell Press, 1978.

Babcock, Barbara. "Taking Liberties, Writing from the Margins and Doing It With Difference." *Journal of American Folklore* 100 (1987), 390-411.

Barolini, Helen. *The Dream Book: An Anthology of Writings by Italian-American Women*. New York: Schocken, 1985.

Bauman, Richard. *Verbal Art as Performance*. Prospect Heights, Illinois: Waveland Press, 1977.

Ben-Amos, Dan, ed. *Folklore Genres*. Austin: University of Texas Press, 1976.

Brunvand, Jan. *The Study of American Folklore: An Introduction*. 2nd ed. New York: W.W. Norton Company, 1978.

Burke, Peter. *Popular Culture in Early Modern Europe*. New York New York University Press, 1978.

Caroli, Betty Boyd, Robert Harney and Lydio Tomassi, eds. *The Italian Immigrant Woman in North America*. Toronto: Multicultural History Society of Ontario, 1978, 273-288.

Cellini, Leo. "Emigration, the Italian Family and Changing Roles." In *The Italian Immigrant Woman in North America*. Eds. Betty Boyd Caroli, Robert Harney and Lydio Tomassi. Toronto: Multicultural History Society of Ontario, 1978.

Coffin, Tristram. P., and Hennig Cohen. *Folklore in America*. New York: Doubleday, 1966.

Cornelisan, Ann. *Women of the Shadows: A Study of Wives and Mothers of Southern Italy*. New York: Vintage Books, 1976.

de Caro, Frances. *Women and Folklore: A Bibliographic Survey*. West Port, Connecticut: Greenwood Press, 1983.

Degh, Linda. *People in the Tobacco Belt: Four Lives*. Ottawa: National Museum of Canada, 1972.

Dolby-Stahl, Sandra K. "A Literary Folkloristic: Methodology for the Study of Meaning in Personal Narrative." *Journal of American Folklore Research* 22(1985), 45-69.

————. *Literary Folkloristics and the Personal Narrative*. Bloomington: Indiana University Press, 1989.

Dorson, Richard, ed. *Folklore and Folklife: An Introduction*. Chicago: University of Chicago Press, 1972.

Falassi, Alessandro. *Folklore by the Fireside: Text and Context of the Tuscan Veglia*. Austin: University of Texas Press, 1980.

Farrer, Claire, ed. *Women and Folklore: Images and Genres*. Prospect Heights, Illinois: Waveland Press, 1975.

Freeman-Cardozo, Inez. "Games Mexican Girls Play." In *Women and Folklore*. Ed. Claire Farrer. Prospects Heights, Illinois: Waveland Press, 1983, 12-25.

Gambino, Richard. *Blood of My Blood: The Dilemma of the Italian-Americans*. New York: Doubleday, 1974. Rpt. Toronto/New York: Guernica Editions, 1996.

Gans, Herbert. *The Urban Villagers: Group and Class in the Life of Italian Americans*. New York: Free Press, 1962.

Glassie, Henry. *The Spirit of Folk Art*. New York: Abrams, 1989; Santa Fe, New Mexico: Museum of International Folk Art, 1989.

Gluck, Sherna Berger and Dahpne Patai, eds. *Women's Words: The Feminist Practice of Oral History*. New York: Routledge Press, 1991.

Hawes, Bess Lomax. "Folksongs and Functions: Some Thoughts on the American Lullaby." *Journal of American Folklore* 87 (1974), 66-71.

Herzfeld, Michael. "Silence, Submission, and Subversion: Toward a Poetics of Womanhood." In *Contested Identities: Gender and Kinship in Modern Greece*. Eds. Peter Loisos and Evthymios Papataxiarchis. New Jersey: Princeton University Press, 1991, 79-97.

Herzfeld, Michael. "Within and Without: The Category of "Female" in the Ethnography of Modern Greece." In *Gender and Power in Rural Greece*. Ed. Jill Dubisch. New Jersey: Princeton University Press, 1986, 215-233.

Kirshenblatt-Gimblett, Barbara. "The Future of Folklore Studies in America: The Urban Frontier." *Folklore Forum* 16 (1983), 175-234.

Iacovetta, Franca. "Trying to Make Ends Meet: An Historical Look at Italian-Canadian Women: The State and Family Survival Strategies in Post War Toronto." *Canadian Women's Studies: Cahiers de la femme* 8, no. 2 (1987), 6-11.

Jahner, Elaine. "Women Remembering Life History as Exemplary Pattern." In *Women's Folklore, Women's Culture*. Eds. Susan Kalcik and Rosan

Ann Jordan Philadelphia: University of Pennsylvania Press, 1985, 214-233.

Johnson, C. L. "The Maternal Role in Contemporary Italian-American Family." In *The Italian Immigrant Woman in North America.* Eds. Betty Boyd Caroli, Robert Harney and Lydio Tomassi. Toronto: Multicultural History Society of Ontario, 1978, 234-246.

Jordan, Rosan Ann. "The Folklore and Ethnic Identity of a Mexican-American Woman." Ph.D. diss., Indiana University, 1976.

Kalcik, Susan. "'. . . like Ann's gynecologist or the time I was almost raped': Personal Narratives in Women's Rap Groups." In *Women and Folklore: Images and Genres.* Ed. Claire Farrer. Prospects Heights, Illinois: Waveland Press, 1975, 3-11.

Kalcik, Susan and Rosan Ann Jordan, eds. *Women's Folklore, Women's Culture.* Philadelphia: University of Pennsylvania Press, 1985.

Levine, Lawrence W. *Black Culture and Black Consciousness.* New York: Oxford Press, 1978.

Lee-Juteau, Danielle and Barbara Roberts. "Ethnicity and Femininity: D'après nos experiences." *Canadian Ethnic Studies* 8, no. 1 (1981), 1-23.

Martin, Bernice. *Sociology of Contemporary Cultural Change.* New York: St. Martin's Press, 1981.

Mascia-Lees, Frances, Patricia Sharpe and Colleen Ballerino Cohen. "The Postmodernist Turn in Anthropology: Cautions from a Feminist Perspective." *Signs* 15 (1989), 7-33.

Mathias, Elizabeth and Richard Raspa. *Italian Folktales in America: The Verbal Art of an Immigrant Woman.* Detroit: Wayne State University Press, 1978.

Minister, Kristina. "Feminist Frame of the Oral History Interview." In *Women' Words: The Feminist Practice of Oral History.* Eds. Sherna Berger Gluck and Dahpne Patai. New York: Routledge Press, 1991.

Myerhoff, Barbara. *Number Our Days.* New York: Simon and Schuster, 1978.

Noether, Emiliana. "The Silent Half: *Le contadine Del Sud* before the First World War." In *The Italian Immigrant Woman in North America.* Eds. Betty Boyd, Caroli, Robert F. Harney and Lydio F. Tomassi. Toronto: Multicultural History Society of Ontario, 1978, 3-22..

Papataxiarchis, Evthymios and Peter Loizes, eds. *Contested Identities: Gender and Kinship in Modern Greece.* Princeton, New Jersey: Princeton University Press, 1991.

Passerini, Luisa. "Women's Personal Narratives: Myths, Experience and Emotions." In *Interpreting Women's Lives: Feminist Theory and Personal Narratives.* Ed. Personal Narrative Group. Bloomington: Indiana University Press, 1987, 189-197.

Passerini, Luisa. *Fascism in Popular Memory*. New York: Cambridge University Press, 1987.

Peristiany, John. *Honour and Shame: The Values of Mediterranean Society*. Chicago: University of Chicago Press, 1966.

Perry, Harriet. "The Metonymic Definition of the Female and the Concept of Honour Among Italian Immigrant Families in Toronto." In *The Italian Immigrant Woman in North America*. Eds. Betty Boyd Caroli, Robert Harney and Lydio Tomassi. Toronto: Multicultural History Society of Ontario, 1978, 224-243.

Portelli, Alessandro. *The Death of Luigi Trastulli and Other Stories: Form and Meaning in Oral History*. Albany: State University of New York Press, 1991.

Radner, Joan N. and Susan Lanser S. "The Feminist Voice: Strategies of Coding in Folklore and Literature." *Journal of American Folklore* 100 (1987), 412-425.

Robinson, John A. "Personal Narrative Reconsidered." *Journal of American Folklore* 94 (1981), 58-85.

Rogers, Carol S. "Good to Think: The 'Peasant' in Contemporary France." *Anthropological Quarterly* 60 (1987), 56-63.

Scarpaci, Vincenza. "Contadina: Plaything of the Middle Class Woman Historian." *Ethnic Studies* 9 (1981), 21-38.

Stoeltje, Beverly. "Introduction: Feminist Revisions." *Journal of Folklore Research* 25 (1988), 146-153.

Tentori, Tullio. "Social Classes in Matera." In *Mediterranean Family Structures*. Ed. John Peristiany. New York: Cambridge Press, 1976, 271-289.

Titon, Jeff. "The Life Story." *Journal of American Folklore* 93 (1980), 276-292.

Webster, Susan K. "Women and Folklore: Performers, Characters, Scholars." *Women's Studies International Forum* 9 (1986), 219-226.

Watson, Lawrence Craig and Maria-Barbara Watson-Franke. *Interpreting Life Histories: An Anthropological Inquiry*. New Brunswick, New Jersey: Rutgers, 1985.

Winsey, Valentine Rosseli. "The Italian Immigrant Women Who Arrived in the United States Before World War I." In *Studies in Italian American Social History*. Ed. Francesco Cordasco. Towtowa, New Jersey: Rowan & Littlefield, 1975, 199-210.

LIST OF PHOTOGRAPHS

Stefania Annibale in her home.

Filomena Azzuolo at her work place.

Antonietta De Fronzo posing underneath a picture of her deceased husband.

Anna Del Negro in her kitchen demonstrating how to carry the traditional Abruzzese water bucket *(conca)*.

Genoveffa Della Zazzera inside a room where there is a home altar with a variety of religious icons.

Graziella Di Corpo at *Centro Donne*.

Francesca Mancini posing in her home.

Genoveffa Della Zazzera praying at her confessional.

All the photographs are by Paul Perry.

Printed and bound
in Canada by
MARC VEILLEUX IMPRIMEUR INC.
in April, 2003